AMELIA ISLAND

TRAVEL GUIDE

2023

The Ultimate Guide to the Best Architecture, Landscapes, History, and Culture of Amelia Island. Explore, Enjoy Tasty Foods, Beautiful Hotels, With Safety/Saving Tips

Darlene M. Keenan

TABLE OF CONTENT

INTRODUCTION

Amelia Island, a lovely tourist island, off the coast of Jacksonville, Florida, drew me with its promises of natural beauty, rich history, and a calm getaway from the hustle and bustle of daily life.

Eager to discover this secret treasure, I set out on a quest that would permanently mark Amelia Island in my heart, but join me as I recall the wonderful moments and magnificent vistas that made my trip on Amelia Island absolutely unforgettable.

As I strolled onto Main Beach's pristine beaches, I was met with a breathtaking panorama of the Atlantic Ocean reaching as far as the eye could see. The lovely sea wind and the rhythmic crashing of the waves quickly took me to a feeling of complete calm.

I spent hours sunning on the smooth beaches, periodically cooling down in the chilly seas. The beaches' unspoilt beauty, such as Peters Point Beachfront Park, provided a calm retreat where I could relax and reconnect with nature.

As I strolled through the streets of Fernandina Beach, Amelia Island's history unfurled before my eyes. The Victorian structures bordering Centre Street provided a vivid depiction of the island's history. I marveled at the well-preserved buildings and lovely businesses that harkened back to a bygone age as I strolled around the historic neighborhood.

The Amelia Island Museum of History offered an enthralling view into the island's history, with artifacts and tales ranging from Timucuan Indians to the Golden Age of Pirates.

Amelia Island cannot be experienced without partaking on its culinary pleasures. I found myself immersed in a gourmet universe, eating fresh seafood specialties at famous waterfront eateries.

The local harvest, which included exquisite shrimp and tasty oysters, attested to the island's maritime riches. I couldn't resist trying interesting meals like charred red snapper and shrimp and grits, which were beautifully cooked to perfection. Every meal was a delectable symphony of flavors that left me wanting more.

Amelia Island's natural splendor revealed itself as I explored its lovely parks and pathways. I was amazed by the moss-draped live oak trees and meandering nature pathways at Fort Clinch State Park. The park's attractiveness was enhanced by the symphony of bird melodies and the occasional sight of a gorgeous deer.

I submerged myself in the tranquil ambience and marveled at the richness of marine life, from lively dolphins to exquisite herons, on a kayak expedition around the island's canals.

To round up my trip, I took use of the island's exquisite amenities. Amelia Island's world-class resorts offered a haven of leisure and indulgence. I indulged in spa treatments that refreshed both my body and mind, enabling the cares of daily life to go away. I discovered a sanctuary of calm beside the poolside, surrounded by lush flora and the soothing sound of waterfalls, offering a genuine getaway from the outer world.

My trip to Amelia Island was a picture of breathtaking vistas, cultural immersion, and beautiful moments of calm. Amelia Island made an unforgettable impression on my spirit, from the gorgeous beaches that encouraged me to relax to the island's fascinating history that grabbed my mind. It is a site where natural beauty and historical legacy meet, providing a refuge of peace for the weary traveler. The charm of Amelia Island will last forever.

About Amelia Island

Amelia Island is an island in northeastern Florida, of the United States. It is recognized for its beautiful beaches, rich history, and natural beauty and is located just off the coast of Jacksonville.

Amelia Island's gorgeous shoreline, which spans for nearly 13 miles, is one of its key draws. The island has a wide range of beaches, from noisy and crowded to isolated and calm. These beaches provide sunbathing, swimming, beachcombing, and a variety of water activities.

Amelia Island has an interesting history dating back to the colonial period. The Timucuan Indians initially settled there, and it eventually became a sanctuary for pirates. The island passed through the hands of various European nations before becoming a part of the United States. Fernandina Beach, on the northern end of the island, has kept most of its historic appeal, with well-preserved Victorian buildings.

Amelia Island is noted for its robust food culture, in addition to its natural beauty and history. The island's eating choices vary from fresh seafood restaurants to expensive diners and informal cafés. Visitors may have delectable meals while admiring the coastal views or seeing the charming downtown area.

Amelia Island has a plethora of activities for outdoor lovers. Visitors may go hiking, bicycling, or animal spotting on the island's golf courses, nature paths, and state parks. Fishing is also popular in the region, offering both freshwater and saltwater options.

Amelia Island provides upscale resorts, spas, and boutique stores for visitors seeking a more relaxing experience. Visitors may indulge in spa treatments, shop at unique shops, or just relax in a tranquil atmosphere.

Overall, Amelia Island is a charming resort that blends natural beauty, a rich history, and a variety of recreational opportunities. Amelia Island provides something for everyone, whether you're looking for a beach vacation, a taste of history, or a peaceful holiday.

History Of Amelia Island

Amelia Island is a historical site in northeastern Florida, United States. It has a varied and intriguing history, with influences from Native American tribes, European colonialism, and strategic significance at various times.

Long before European migrants arrived, Amelia Island was home to many Native American tribes, notably the Timucua. They flourished in the region for thousands of years, surviving on the island's bountiful natural resources.

Amelia Island was a source of strife between the Spanish, British, and French during the 17th and 18th centuries. It was a sanctuary for pirates and privateers who utilized the island's strategic position to launch assaults on passing ships.

Luis Aury, who built a base on Amelia Island in the early nineteenth century, was the most notorious pirate linked with the island.

A group of American rebels known as the "Patriots of Amelia Island" temporarily took possession of the island from the Spanish in 1817. Their objective was to form an independent republic, but their uprising was short-lived, and the Spanish quickly recovered control.

Amelia Island became a location for the clandestine slave trade in the early nineteenth century. Enslaved Africans were brought to the island by smugglers, where they were sold and transferred to other regions of the United States. This illegal commerce was carried on until the American Civil War.

Amelia Island eventually turned into a vacation area after the Civil War. Its natural beauty, moderate temperature, and immaculate beaches drew travelers looking for leisure and pleasure. Many expensive hotels and resorts were constructed, including the well-known Ritz-Carlton, which opened in 1991 and remains a significant feature on the island.

Amelia Island is recognized today for its historic beauty, magnificent beaches, and thriving community. The island's town of Fernandina Beach is on the National Register of Historic Places and has well-preserved Victorian architecture. The Amelia Island Concours d'Elegance, a prominent vintage vehicle display, is one of the island's yearly festivities.

Amelia Island's history, which ranges from Native American colonies through colonial wars, piracy, and its metamorphosis into a major tourist destination, making it an enthralling site for both locals and tourists interested in learning about the past.

CHAPTER ONE

PLANNING YOUR TRIP TO AMELIA ISLAND

When To Visit Amelia Island

Several things might impact your decision on the ideal time to visit Amelia Island. Timing may dramatically improve your experience on the island, from weather and crowd levels to seasonal events and activities. Here's an overview of the many seasons on Amelia Island to help you decide when to visit:

From March to May:

Amelia Island is especially beautiful in the spring. Temperatures begin to rise, ranging from the mid-60s to the mid-80s Fahrenheit (18-29°C). It's an ideal time to discover the island's natural beauty, participate in outdoor activities, and enjoy the mild weather. Beautiful flowering flowers and a feeling of regeneration accompany the spring season. However, spring break may draw more visitors, resulting in somewhat higher lodging fees and more crowds.

Summer months (June through August):

Summer temperatures on Amelia Island range from the low 70s to the mid-90s Fahrenheit (21-35°C). It's a popular season for beachgoers, water sports aficionados, and vacationing families.

The turquoise seas of the island's immaculate beaches beckon, and the long days allow for plenty of outdoor activities. Remember that summers may be humid, and that afternoon rains are typical. Because of the busy tourist season, it is best to book hotels and activities in advance.

Autumn (September-November):

Autumn is a lovely and relatively peaceful season to visit Amelia Island. Temperatures continue to fall, with temperatures ranging from the mid-60s to the mid-80s Fahrenheit (18-29°C).

The humidity drops, making outdoor activities more pleasant. Autumn also provides lovely winds and vivid foliage, making for a beautiful background for exploring the island. Furthermore, you may get better discounts on lodging during this shoulder season, and there are less people than during the summer.

From December until February:

Amelia Island's winters are warm, with temperatures averaging in the 50s and 60s Fahrenheit (10-15°C). While it may not be usual beach season, it is great for people looking for a serene and tranquil escape.

Winter delivers a calm atmosphere, enabling visitors to enjoy uncrowded beaches, learn about the island's history and attractions, and engage in comfortable interior activities. Some events and festivals, such as holiday festivities and Amelia Island Restaurant Week, take place throughout the winter months.

Aside from seasonal considerations, you should think about any special events or activities you want to engage in during your vacation to Amelia Island.

Throughout the year, the island holds a variety of events, including the Amelia Island Concours d'Elegance (spring), the Isle of Eight Flags Shrimp Festival (spring), and the Amelia Island Chamber Music Festival (winter). These events may provide you with one-of-a-kind experiences, but they may also have an influence on hotel availability and costs.

Finally, the optimum time to visit Amelia Island is determined by your interests and priorities. Whether you're looking for sunny beach days, outdoor experiences, or a tranquil getaway, each season has its own attraction. You may select the best time to come and make treasured memories on our gorgeous island refuge by taking into account the weather, crowd levels, and any desired events.

How To Get To Amelia Island

Amelia Island, located off the northeastern coast of Florida, entices visitors with its picturesque attractiveness, beautiful beaches, and rich history. This mesmerizing island paradise provides something for everyone, whether you're looking for a quiet holiday or an adventure-filled getaway. Set off on an exciting trip as we show you how to get to Amelia Island and reveal the charming road that takes you to this hidden jewel.

By Air:

Jacksonville International Airport (JAX) is the nearest major airport to Amelia Island, located roughly 30 miles southwest of the island. JAX provides easy access to Amelia Island, with multiple domestic and international flights. You may hire a vehicle or arrange for a shuttle service to take you to your destination from the airport.

By Car:

Amelia Island is readily accessible through various motorways if you prefer a picturesque road trip. Interstate 95 (I-95) links major East Coast towns, and Exit 373 onto A1A/SR 200 East will take you straight to the island. The route passes through stunning scenery, lovely coastal villages, and lush wetlands.

Traveling by Boat:

Amelia Island welcomes boaters with open arms if they have a passion for marine activities. The island has marinas and docking facilities, making it a popular sailing destination. Whether you have your own boat or choose to hire one, you may reach the island's coastlines by navigating the Intracoastal Waterway or the Atlantic Ocean.

By Ferry :

Consider riding the boat from Mayport to Fernandina Beach for a unique and relaxing experience. This gorgeous cruise, operated by the St. Johns River Ferry, enables you to take in the breathtaking vistas of the river and shoreline as you glide approach Amelia Island. When you depart, you'll be engulfed in the mesmerizing ambience of the island.

By Train:

Train aficionados may reach Amelia Island through Amtrak. The closest Amtrak station is in Jacksonville, FL (JAX), which has connections to locations all throughout the United States. You may then hire a vehicle or use other modes of transportation to the last stage of your trip to Amelia Island.

It's easy to navigate Amelia Island's attractive spots once you've arrived. There are rental vehicle businesses at the airport and in Fernandina Beach, the island's principal town. Alternatively, you may explore the island by renting a bicycle from one of numerous stores. There are also local taxis and ride-sharing services.

Traveling to Amelia Island is an intriguing experience that captivates the senses from the start. The journey to this hidden jewel is packed with suspense and surprise, whether you want to fly, drive, sail, or even take a boat.

When you arrive on the island, you will be welcomed by the natural beauty of its beaches, the kindness of its population, and the rich history that pervades every area. Amelia Island awaits your arrival, eager to provide an incredible retreat that will leave you yearning for more.

The Easiest Ways Of Get Around Amelia Island

Exploring Amelia Island is a great experience since it provides a variety of practical and entertaining modes of transportation. Here are the finest methods to get about Amelia Island, from its beautiful neighborhoods to its magnificent coastline:

Car Rental:

Visitors who want the independence and flexibility of seeing the island at their own leisure sometimes rent a vehicle. There are many vehicle rental firms near Jacksonville International Airport (JAX) and in Fernandina Beach. You can easily visit the island's attractions, beaches, and hidden secrets with a rental vehicle, making it a perfect choice for families and people planning day getaways.

Bicycles:

With its topography and gorgeous bike trails, Amelia Island is a cyclist's dream. There are several rental establishments that provide bicycles for people of all ages, including beach cruisers, tandems, and even electric bikes. Pedal through the lovely streets of Fernandina Beach, pedal through historic downtown Fernandina Beach, or take a leisurely ride along the coast, soaking in the cool sea air and stunning sights.

Carts for golf:

Consider hiring a golf cart to really immerse yourself in the island's laid-back culture. This enjoyable and environmentally safe means of transportation lets you easily tour Amelia Island while enjoying the open-air experience. Golf cart rentals come in a variety of sizes and may suit small groups or families. Cruise around Fernandina Beach's streets, visiting stores and restaurants and discovering secret nooks and crannies that might be overlooked on foot.

Walking:

Because of its tiny size and pedestrian-friendly streets, Amelia Island is a perfect place for exploring on foot. Stroll around Fernandina Beach's historic neighborhood, which is lined with Victorian-era mansions and beautiful businesses. Discover the island's rich history, visit art galleries, dine at local restaurants, and absorb in the inviting atmosphere at your leisure.

Taxis and Ride-Hailing Companies:

Taxis and ridesharing services are widely accessible on Amelia Island if you choose not to drive or walk. Local taxi companies are available in Fernandina Beach, providing handy transportation for shorter distances or for returning to your resort after a day of exploring. Rideshare services like Uber and Lyft are also available on the island, giving a simple and dependable way to get about.

Public Transportation:

Amelia Island has a modest public transportation system called NassauTRANSIT. This bus service links many areas of the island, including Fernandina Beach, the seaside region, and significant hotels. While the service has limited operating hours and routes, it may be a cost-effective way to travel about, especially for guests staying in core regions.

Because of the island's small size and variety of transportation choices, getting about Amelia Island is a snap. Whether you hire a vehicle for convenience, get on a bicycle for a leisurely ride, or explore the island on foot to immerse yourself in its beauty, each means of transportation offers a distinct experience.

Amelia Island awaits your exploration, delivering unique experiences at every turn, from the tiny town of Fernandina Beach to the beautiful beaches.

Choosing the Best Amelia Island Accommodations

Amelia Island provides a diverse range of hotels to suit any traveler's needs. The island offers a diverse range of accommodations, from opulent beachfront resorts to lovely bed & breakfasts, ensuring a memorable and pleasant visit.

Join me as we explore the art of selecting the ideal lodgings on Amelia Island, where relaxation and refreshment await.

Beachfront Hotels:

Amelia Island's beachfront resorts are an excellent alternative for anyone looking for a traditional beach experience. These resorts give an unrivaled coastal retreat, with breathtaking ocean views, direct beach access, and a variety of facilities.

Indulge in lavish spa treatments, dine on fine cuisine, and relax by sparkling pools while just steps away from the sun-drenched beaches. Beachfront resorts are the essence of coastal enjoyment, with world-class service and a plethora of activities.

Bed & Breakfasts and Historic Inns:

Stay at one of Amelia Island's historic inns or bed & breakfasts to immerse yourself in the island's rich history and beautiful environment. These tiny apartments provide a distinct combination of contemporary conveniences and old-world charm. Enjoy individualized service, nicely decorated accommodations, and delectable prepared breakfasts. Many of these hotels are located in renovated Victorian houses, giving your stay an added touch of luxury and charm.

Condos and vacation rentals:

Vacation rentals and condominiums are a fantastic alternative for individuals looking for a home-away-from-home experience. Amelia Island offers a variety of vacation rentals, from modest beach cottages to luxurious complexes.

These accommodations are ideal for families or groups since they often have numerous bedrooms, living spaces, and fully equipped kitchens. Enjoy the flexibility to prepare your own meals, relax in your own space, and enjoy the luxuries of a genuine home while exploring the island's wonderful surroundings.

Boutique Inns:

Amelia Island is well-known for its boutique hotels, which combine individual service with distinctive design. These smaller-scale venues provide a pleasant and personal ambience, often showing local artwork and combining aspects of island culture.

Boutique hotels provide a unique combination of comfort, elegance, and originality, making them a fantastic alternative for guests looking for a more customized experience.

Resorts that provide golf and spa services:

Amelia Island is a well-known golf and spa destination, with various facilities catering exclusively to these interests. These hotels have world-class golf courses created by famous architects, giving golf aficionados of all skill levels with an unforgettable experience.

Furthermore, revitalizing spas provide a variety of treatments and wellness programs that enable customers to rest and unwind in a calm location. These resorts are ideal for anyone looking for a break that blends relaxation, recreation, and pampering.

Choosing the appropriate Amelia Island lodgings is an important part of creating a great vacation.

Whether you choose a magnificent beachside resort, a lovely old inn, a vacation rental, a boutique hotel, or a resort with golf and spa amenities, the island has something for everyone.

You'll be engulfed in luxury, warmth, and the island's distinct charm the minute you set foot in your selected lodgings. Allow Amelia Island to be your refuge, where dreams come true and the ideal hideaway awaits you.

What To Pack To Amelia Island

Packing for a vacation to Amelia Island requires careful consideration of the island's tropical temperature, relaxed environment, and variety of activities. To help you plan your trip, here's a comprehensive list of things to bring for a wonderful stay on Amelia Island:

Clothing:

Pack a variety of shorts, t-shirts, tank tops, and sundresses to keep comfortable in the island's warm weather.

swimwear: Bring your favorite swimwear to enjoy the beautiful beaches and resort pools.

Cover-ups and sarongs are important for shifting from the beach to restaurants or seeing the island's attractions.

While Amelia Island sees pleasant temps, nights may be cold, so bring a light jacket or sweater for extra comfort.

Bring a pair of good walking shoes to explore the island's picturesque neighborhoods, natural paths, and historic attractions. For the beach, wear sandals or flip-flops.

Hat and sunglasses: Pack a wide-brimmed hat and sunglasses to protect yourself from the sun.

Beach necessities:

Beach towel: While some lodgings supply beach towels, having an extra one for your beach adventures is always a good idea.

Sunscreen: Bring sunscreen with a high SPF to protect your skin from the harsh Florida sun.

Beach bag: Pack your basics, such as sunscreen, drink, snacks, and reading material, in a large beach bag.

Beach umbrella or sunshade: For additional shade on your beach outings, pack a portable beach umbrella or sunshade.

Snorkeling equipment and water toys: Bring your own snorkeling equipment if you wish to explore the island's underwater ecosystem. Inflatable water toys may also make your beach experiences more enjoyable.

Outdoor Recreation:

Insect protection: Although Amelia Island has less bugs than other places, it's always a good idea to bring insect repellant, particularly if you intend on trekking or visiting nature paths.

If you're going on an outdoor adventure, bring a daypack or backpack to carry basics like water, food, a camera, and additional clothes.

Binoculars: If you like bird watching or observing animals, bring a pair of binoculars with you to improve your experience.

Items of Interest:

Camera and/or smartphone: Use your camera or smartphone to capture the amazing moments and breathtaking views of Amelia Island.

Portable chargers and adapters: Bring a portable charger to keep your gadgets charged while on the road. If you are going from a country other than the United States, please be sure you have the proper power adapters.

Reusable water bottle: Carry a reusable water bottle to stay hydrated. Amelia Island has plenty of water refill stations, so you can stay hydrated all day.

Travel documents and necessities:

Valid ID or passport: For travel, make sure you have a valid form of identification or passport.

Consider obtaining travel insurance to protect yourself from unanticipated occurrences.

Copies of key papers: Bring duplicates of your vacation itinerary, hotel bookings, and any other necessary paperwork. It's also a good idea to save electronic copies on the cloud or email them to yourself for quick access.

Cash and credit cards: Bring a combination of cash and credit cards for transactions, since some smaller businesses may prefer cash.

Remember that Amelia Island has various supermarkets and shops where you may pick up any goods you neglected to bring. You'll be well-prepared to enjoy the island's tropical beauty, outdoor experiences, and laid back environment if you bring the necessities listed above. Best wishes for your trip to Amelia Island!

Visa and Entry Requirements to Amelia Island

A vacation to Amelia Island is an exciting possibility, and knowing the visa and admission procedures is an important aspect of preparing your trip.

Amelia Island, located in the United States, attracts people from all over the globe to enjoy its beautiful beaches, attractive neighborhoods, and engaging culture. Join us as we unpack the visa and entrance formalities to ensure a smooth and flawless journey to this tropical paradise.

VWP (Visa Waiver Program):

The Visa Waiver Program (VWP) allows tourists from qualified countries to visit Amelia Island without needing a visa. Visitors may remain in the United States for up to 90 days for tourist or business reasons under the VWP.

Travelers must apply for and acquire authorisation via the Electronic System for Travel authorisation (ESTA) before their journey. The ESTA application may be completed online for a minimal charge.

B-2 Visitor Visa:

If you are not qualified for the Visa Waiver Program or want to remain for more than 90 days, you may need to apply for a Visitor Visa (B-2). The B-2 visa is appropriate for visitors to the United States for tourism, vacation, or medical treatment.

To acquire a B-2 visa, make an appointment at the closest US embassy or consulate in your native country. Completing the relevant forms, presenting supporting papers, attending an interview, and paying the application cost are all part of the application procedure.

Passport Information:

All visitors to Amelia Island, regardless of visa type, must have a valid passport. Your passport should be valid for at least six months after you plan to leave the United States. Make sure your passport has enough vacant pages for immigration stamps and any visas that may be required.

Immigration and Customs:

At your initial point of entry into the United States, you will go through customs and immigration. Prepare to show your passport, customs declaration form, and any supporting documentation, such as your ESTA authorisation or B-2 visa.

Customs agents may inquire about the purpose of your visit, the length of your stay, and evidence of lodging or a return ticket. To minimize problems, it is critical to respond accurately and supply correct information.

COVID-19 Travel Requirements:

Given the continuing COVID-19 epidemic, it is critical to remain up to current on the most recent travel recommendations and limitations. Check the official websites of the United States government, the

Centers for Disease Control and Prevention (CDC), and local health authorities before visiting Amelia Island for any travel warnings, testing requirements, or quarantine processes that may be in effect.

Additionally, ensure that you have all of the relevant documents, such as immunization records or negative COVID-19 test results, as requested by the authorities.

As you plan your trip to Amelia Island, familiarize yourself with the visa and entrance procedures to ensure a smooth and happy vacation. Whether you qualify for the Visa Waiver Program or need to apply for a Visitor Visa, it is essential that your passport is valid and that you follow customs and immigration procedures.

Keep up to date on any travel advisories relating to the current epidemic, since they may affect your trip plans. You may confidently step foot on Amelia Island with the appropriate preparations in place, ready to appreciate the island's beauty, charm, and friendly welcome.

Currency And Language of Amelia Island

Currency:
The United States Dollar (USD) is the official currency of Amelia Island and the whole United States. It is recommended that visitors to Amelia Island bring several US dollars in cash for modest purchases and transactions. At airports, banks, and currency exchange offices, you may quickly swap your currency for US dollars.

Most Amelia Island establishments, including hotels, restaurants, and stores, accept major credit cards including Visa, Mastercard, and American Express. ATMs are generally accessible as well, enabling you to withdraw cash in US dollars if necessary.

Language:
English is the major language spoken on Amelia Island, as it is across the United States. The official language is English, which is widely known and spoken by the local populace. When conversing with residents, hotel employees, or participating in everyday activities, you will see that English is the prevalent language.

Amelia Island welcomes travelers from all over the globe, and you may come across multilingual employees at hotels, tourist sites, and famous tourist places who can help you in a variety of languages. However, having a basic command of English is useful for navigating the island and communicating efficiently with locals.

If you are not proficient in English, having a pocket-sized English language phrasebook or translation software on your smartphone may help with basic communication. To accommodate to the varied spectrum of tourists, the island's tourism office and visitor centers are often staffed with people who can give information and help in several languages.

Having US Dollars as the native currency while visiting Amelia Island will guarantee seamless transactions. Because English is the most often spoken language on the island, knowing basic English phrases and having translation tools will improve your experience and facilitate conversation.

On Amelia Island, embrace the island's warm and welcoming environment as you explore its natural beauties, interact with the inhabitants, and make lifelong memories.

Suggested Budget for Tourists to Amelia Island

To guarantee a pleasurable and stress-free holiday, consider your budget while planning a trip to Amelia Island. From lodging and transportation to food and activities, a recommended budget for travellers visiting this picturesque island is necessary. Here's a comprehensive guide to planning your expenses for a wonderful vacation to Amelia Island:

Accommodation:
The price of lodging on Amelia Island varies according to the nature and location of the resort. Beachfront resorts and luxury hotels often charge higher prices, whilst budget-friendly choices such as vacation rentals, bed & breakfasts, and boutique hotels provide more reasonable options.
Expect to pay between $150 and $300 per night on average for mid-range lodging. Prices, however, may vary based on the season and demand.

Transportation:
If you want to travel to Amelia Island, the closest major airport is Jacksonville International Airport (JAX), which is about 30 miles

southwest of the island. To get to Amelia Island, you may hire a vehicle, use a cab, or arrange for a shuttle service from the airport.

Renting a vehicle allows you to explore the island and its surroundings in comfort and freedom. Prices for daily automobile rentals begin about $40, however charges may vary based on the vehicle type and rental period.

Dining:

Amelia Island has a rich food scene with alternatives for all tastes and budgets. Prices for dining may vary from inexpensive informal cafes to fancy establishments.

A dinner at a mid-range restaurant may often cost between $10 and $20, but elite eating facilities may charge $30 or more per person. Exploring local seafood delicacies and regional cuisine may create a one-of-a-kind culinary experience.

Attractions and Activities:

Amelia Island has a plethora of activities and attractions to satisfy a wide range of interests. There are alternatives for any budget, whether you want to explore the island's natural beauty, historic monuments, or participate in water activities. Here are some rough estimates for popular activities:

Admission to state parks is $5 to $6 per car:

Boat cruises and excursions cost from $30 and $100 per person, depending on the length and kind of tour.

Golf: Prices vary based on the course, but a round of golf should cost between $50 and $150.

Prices for spa treatments vary from $100 to $200 or more, depending on the services and length.

Expenses Not Listed:

Budget for extra charges such as parking fees, gratuities, souvenirs, and unplanned costs. A reasonable rule of thumb is to put aside 10% to 20% of your total budget for these incidental items.

While the advised price for a vacation to Amelia Island varies based on personal tastes and the length of your stay, a mid-range budget would be roughly $150 to $300 per day, excluding flights.

When calculating your budget, keep in mind to account for lodging, transportation, meals, activities, and other costs. You may make the most of your time on Amelia Island while also assuring a stress-free and joyful holiday experience if you have a clear concept of your budgetary expectations.

Money Saving Tips in
Amelia Island

A journey to Amelia Island does not have to be expensive. You can make your ideal trip a reality while keeping within your budget with a little study and wise decision-making.

We've created an exhaustive list of money-saving recommendations to help you make the most of your stay on this gorgeous island paradise, from locating economical hotels to enjoying budget-friendly activities.

Timing:

Consider visiting Amelia Island during the off-season, such as late spring or early autumn, when lodging costs are often cheaper. Furthermore, weekdays often provide greater prices than weekends. You may take advantage of lower pricing while still enjoying the island's charm and beauty if you schedule your vacation during these times.

Check Out Alternatives for Accommodation:

While seaside resorts and luxury hotels are appealing, looking into alternate lodging alternatives might help you save money. Look for vacation rentals, bed &

breakfasts, or guesthouses, which can provide a more intimate and genuine experience at a reduced cost. Websites and applications like Airbnb, VRBO, and Booking.com may assist you in locating economical solutions that meet your requirements and budget.

Eat Like a Local:

Amelia Island has a wide range of eating alternatives to suit all budgets. Explore local restaurants, food trucks, and casual eating venues to save money on meals. These hidden treasures often provide tasty food at lower costs than posh establishments.

Don't be hesitant to ask locals for recommendations—they'll be able to lead you in the right direction for great and affordable meals.

Embrace the Great Outdoors:

Amelia Island's natural beauty is one of its main charms, and thankfully, many outdoor activities are inexpensive or free. Spend your days discovering the island's beautiful beaches, hiking paths, and parks.

Pack a picnic lunch and enjoy a picturesque meal among the island's breathtaking scenery. Take use of certain lodgings' complementary facilities, such as bicycles or kayaks, to improve your outdoor excursions without paying additional money.

Look for low-cost or free entertainment:

Amelia Island is packed with cultural and historical attractions that won't break the bank. Visit Fort Clinch State Park, where the admission cost is low in comparison to the pleasures available.

Attend local festivals, art exhibits, or outdoor concerts, which are often free or have low entrance fees. To learn about forthcoming activities on the island, see the event calendar.

Benefit from Package Deals:

Look for package offers and discounts that incorporate lodging, transportation, and activities. Some hotels and resorts provide special packages that include benefits such as reduced prices, free breakfast, or complementary activities. You may often save money and get additional perks during your stay by combining your costs.

Prepare and plan:

Create a budget before your trip and allot monies for various components of your holiday, such as lodging, transportation, food, and activities.

To locate the greatest rates on attractions, excursions, and rentals, do your homework and check costs ahead of time. You may make educated selections and prevent impulsive spending by planning and preparing.

Use Local Resources:

When you get on the island, go to the visitor center or tourism office to learn about free or low-cost activities, coupons, and discounts offered to travelers. They may give vital insight into cost-effective solutions and assist you in making the most of your stay on Amelia Island.

A budget-friendly trip to Amelia Island is not only doable, but also quite rewarding. By following these money-saving suggestions, you may enjoy all the island has to offer while staying within your budget. Amelia Island may be both economical and fun, from choosing affordable lodgings to discovering natural beauties and taking use of local services.

Best Places to Book Your Amelia Island As a Tourist

Planning a vacation to Amelia Island is an exciting undertaking, and selecting the correct platform or agency to book your trip is critical for a pleasant and memorable experience.

Choosing the correct booking platform may make a major impact in everything from getting the cheapest airfare fares to obtaining lodgings that meet your needs. Join us as we look at the best locations to plan your trip to Amelia Island to ensure a smooth and pleasurable visit.

OTAs (Online Travel Agencies):

Online travel companies are popular platforms that provide a variety of travel services such as flights, lodging, and vehicle rentals. Expedia, Booking.com, and Kayak, among others, provide extensive alternatives for organizing your vacation to Amelia Island.

These portals enable you to compare pricing, read reviews from other travelers, and often offer reduced rates or package offers.

Tourism Official Websites:

Visiting Amelia Island's official tourist website is an excellent method to get accurate and up-to-date information about the island's attractions, lodgings, and activities. These websites often provide special specials, unique discounts, and tourist-specific itineraries. The website of the Amelia Island Tourist Development Council (ameliavisit.com) is a credible source for trip planning and may give direct access to trusted booking partners.

Websites for Hotels and Resorts:

If you have a certain hotel or resort in mind for your stay on Amelia Island, you should go straight to their official website. For direct reservations, many hotels and resorts offer reasonable pricing and special discounts.

When you book directly via their website, you may be able to take advantage of extra amenities such as complimentary breakfast, hotel upgrades, and flexible cancellation policies. Remember to join up for their loyalty programs, which may bring additional savings and privileges.

Platforms for Vacation Rentals:

Vacation rental services such as Airbnb, VRBO, and HomeAway provide a large range of homes on Amelia Island for people looking for a more customized and autonomous experience. These sites enable you to search for a variety of lodgings, ranging from tiny coastal cottages to big complexes.

You may interact with property owners directly, check visitor reviews, and typically discover lower price alternatives, particularly for longer stays or bigger groups.

Travel Agents with Specialties:

Travel specialists that specialize in certain kinds of travel or specialty experiences may provide personalized advice and knowledge. These agencies may specialize in golf trips, eco-tourism, or luxury getaways. They can assist you in creating a one-of-a-kind and memorable vacation to Amelia Island by utilizing their experience and contacts.

Online Travel Forums & Communities:

Participating in internet forums and travel groups may be a great resource while planning a trip to Amelia Island. Websites such as TripAdvisor, Lonely Planet's Thorn Tree Forum, and Reddit's travel subreddits enable you to interact with other travelers, get advice, and learn from their own experiences. Insider tips, recommendations, and ideas for getting the greatest bargains on flights, lodgings, and activities are often shared in these networks.

When planning a trip to Amelia Island, consider combining online travel agencies, official tourist websites, hotel and resort platforms, vacation rental platforms, specialist travel agents, and online travel forums to discover the best alternatives that meet your interests and budget.

Whether you want a full package or a more tailored experience, these platforms provide a plethora of tools and chances to plan the ideal vacation to Amelia Island. With the proper booking partner, you may open the door to this wonderful island and create lasting memories of your stay there.

CHAPTER TWO

AMELIA ISLAND'S TOP ATTRACTIONS

Amelia Island is rich in natural beauty, historical charm, and cultural attractions. From breathtaking beaches to interesting sites, here is a list of must-see things during your visit:

State Park of Fort Clinch:

At Fort Clinch State Park, you may immerse yourself in history. This well-preserved nineteenth-century fort provides guided tours, living history displays, and fascinating exhibits.

Explore the fort's walls, see cannon firings, and wander along the park's picturesque nature paths and pristine beaches.

State Park of Amelia Island:

Discover Amelia Island State Park, a scenic length of coastline with sand dunes, maritime woods, and salt marshes. Walk or bike the park's paths, go shelling, or just relax on the uncrowded beaches while admiring the Atlantic Ocean.

Downtown Fernandina Beach's Historic District:

Take a step back in time as you stroll around Fernandina Beach's historic quarter. Explore the charming stores and boutiques and eat wonderful food at the local restaurants while admiring the well-preserved Victorian-era architecture. Centre Street, the core of downtown, is filled with attractive businesses and lively street activity.

Amelia Island History Museum:

The Amelia Island Museum of History will take you on a journey through the island's rich history. This interesting museum near Fernandina Beach has displays on the island's Native American origins, Spanish colonization, pirate mythology, and the Gilded Age. Take a guided tour to uncover amazing historical tales.

Cumberland Island National Seashore (Kentucky):

Although not officially on Amelia Island, a trip to adjacent Cumberland Island is a once-in-a-lifetime event. This protected area, accessible by boat, has beautiful beaches, old oak trees, and historic ruins. Keep a look out for free-roaming wild horses, which give a magical touch to the island's natural beauty.

Greenway along Egans Creek:

The Egans Creek Greenway, a gorgeous nature preserve with walking pathways, birding opportunities, and vistas of marshland species, will appeal to nature lovers. Explore the well-kept walkways and absorb in the serene atmosphere as you explore the island's natural beauties.

Museum of the American Beach:

Learn about the historical importance of American Beach, a prominent meeting spot for African Americans during the period of segregation, at the American Beach Museum. Discover the community's tales and contributions via exhibitions and artifacts that illustrate the area's cultural legacy.

Plantation on Amelia Island:

The Amelia Island Plantation is a must-see for visitors looking for a premium resort experience. This opulent resort has world-class golf courses, beautiful beaches, a world-class spa, and a range of culinary choices. Take leisurely stroll across the gorgeous gardens or relax yourself with spa treatments.

Horseback Riding on Amelia Island:

With guided horseback riding trips, you can experience the beauty of Amelia Island's beaches on horseback. As you ride along the sandy coastlines, you may explore the shoreline and take in the amazing vistas. It's an incredible way to interact with nature and make memories that will last a lifetime.

Market in Fernandina Beach:

If you come on a Saturday, don't miss the Fernandina Beach MarketPlace, a bustling farmers market with fresh food, artisan goods, and live music. Enjoy fresh and delectable snacks while taking in the welcoming ambiance.

Amelia Island's attractions provide the ideal balance of history, nature, and leisure. These top attractions will provide a riveting and unforgettable experience throughout your stay, whether you're researching the island's interesting heritage, experiencing outdoor activities, or soaking in opulent facilities.

Fort Clinch State Park

Fort Clinch State Park, located on Amelia Island's northern point, is a tribute to both history and natural beauty. The park, with its well-preserved 19th-century fort, beautiful beaches, and different ecosystems, provides visitors with a once-in-a-lifetime chance to immerse themselves in the island's rich legacy and stunning natural surroundings.

Join us as we explore the enthralling world of Fort Clinch State Park, where history and natural beauty live peacefully.

A Look Back in Time:
Fort Clinch was established in the mid-1800s to guard the crucial mouth of the St. Marys River and was named for General Duncan Lamont Clinch. Within the state park, the fort is now a beautifully preserved historic monument.

Take a guided tour of its halls, chambers, and casemates as skilled reenactors bring history to life. Discover the sights and sounds of everyday life in the fort, as well as military exercises and information on the troops who formerly lived here.

Demonstrations of Living History:
Visiting Fort Clinch State Park provides a once-in-a-lifetime chance to see live historical demonstrations. See professional reenactors demonstrate historical tasks including blacksmithing, musket fire, and artillery exercises. Visitors may learn about the everyday lives and military procedures of the men who served at Fort Clinch via these interactive presentations.

Trails in the Wilderness:
Beyond the historic features of the fort, Fort Clinch State Park is a refuge for wildlife lovers. The park is around 1,400 acres in size and has a variety of habitats to explore. Wander amid maritime hammocks, coastal dunes, and salt marshes on the park's natural paths. Keep a

look out for herons, egrets, ospreys, and woodpeckers, among other bird species. The park is also home to wildlife such as gopher tortoises, deer, and armadillos.

Beautiful Beaches:

Fort Clinch State Park has three miles of unspoilt Atlantic Ocean beaches. Sink your toes into the smooth, white sand, take a refreshing plunge in the water, or just rest while soaking up the rays of the sun.

The uncrowded beaches provide a calm environment for beachcombing, shelling, picnics, or strolling along the coast. Before entering the water, verify the park's swimming restrictions and any cautions.

Recreational Activities with Fishing:

Within the park, anglers will have plenty of opportunity to throw their lines. The park has a variety of fishing sites, whether you want to surf fish along the beach or try your luck in the salt marshes.

Anglers may anticipate catching a variety of species such as flounder, redfish, trout, and sheepshead. The park also has picnic spots, a playground, and plenty of room for outdoor activities including bicycling, hiking, and wildlife photography.

Overnight Camping and Stays:

Fort Clinch State Park provides a one-of-a-kind camping experience in the midst of nature. The park has a campground with 69 campsites that include power and water connections, as well as restrooms and showers. Wake up to the sounds of nature, hike the park's paths at daybreak, and spend the evening over a campfire. Reservations are strongly advised, particularly during high seasons.

Amelia Island's Fort Clinch State Park perfectly blends history, natural beauty, and recreational options. Whether you're exploring the fort's rich history, relaxing on the beaches, or immersing yourself in the varied culture.

Amelia Island State Park

Amelia Island State Park, situated on the island's southern tip, is a coastal jewel that provides tourists with an escape into undisturbed natural splendor.

The park's unspoilt beaches, colorful dunes, and different ecosystems offer a calm backdrop for outdoor enthusiasts, nature lovers, and those seeking a reprieve from the rush and bustle of daily life. Join us as we discover Amelia Island State Park's stunning beauties and distinctive charms.

Beautiful Beaches:
Amelia Island State Park spans
over 200 acres and has miles of
unspoilt, sandy beaches that attract
tourists with their tranquil beauty.
Stroll down the beach, dip your
toes in the soft sand, or just sit
back and relax while listening to
the calming sounds of the ocean
waves.

The park's uncrowded beaches
provide a tranquil and isolated
location ideal for sunbathing,
picnics, shelling, or swimming in
the pristine Atlantic seas.

Dunes System:
Amelia Island State Park is home
to a thriving and diversified dune
system that supports a broad
variety of plant and animal species.
These sand dunes serve an
important function in safeguarding
the island's biodiversity and acting
as an erosion barrier.

Admire the park's dramatic
environment of undulating dunes
covered with sea oats, beach
sunflowers, and other coastal
plants as you explore it.

**Birdwatching and wildlife
viewing:**
The plethora of animals that
flourishes inside Amelia Island
State Park will please nature
aficionados. Keep a look out for
gopher tortoises, armadillos, and
ghost crabs as they scurry across
the dunes and coastal vegetation.

The park is also a birdwatcher's paradise, with several kinds of shorebirds, wading birds, and migrating birds visiting. You may identify herons, egrets, ospreys, and even the rare painted bunting using binoculars.

Boardwalks and nature trails:
Explore the park's well-maintained nature paths and boardwalks to immerse yourself in its natural delights. These paths, which wind through maritime hammocks, coastal dunes, and salt marshes, allow visitors to get up close and personal with the area's distinctive flora and animals.

The park's different ecosystems provide visitors the chance to learn about the delicate balance of coastal habitats and their relevance in preserving the island's natural integrity.

Fishing and kayaking:
Amelia Island State Park's surrounding waterways provide great kayaking and fishing possibilities. Paddle across the tranquil salt marshes, watching the beautiful coastal ecology develop in front of you. Anglers may throw from the beach or send kayaks into the sea to explore the numerous fishing sites. These excellent fishing areas are home to a variety of species, including redfish, trout, flounder, and sheepshead.

Programs for Environmental Education and Interpretation:

The park provides educational programs and informative displays to help visitors better appreciate Amelia Island's natural and cultural history.

Take guided nature walks, birding excursions, or themed presentations about the park's ecology, history, and conservation activities. These engaging experiences help visitors get a better understanding of the park's distinctive characteristics and the necessity of protecting its natural resources.

Amelia Island State Park is a coastal paradise where tourists may immerse themselves in the natural splendor of Florida's coast.

From the pristine beaches to the lively dune system and rich animals, the park provides a haven of peace and natural beauty. Whether you want to spend a calm day by the sea, an exciting kayak trip, or an opportunity to connect with nature, we have it all.

Historic Downtown
Fernandina Beach

Historic Downtown Fernandina Beach, situated on Florida's Amelia Island, is a compelling location with old-world charm and a rich history. This attractive downtown center, lined with well-preserved Victorian-era buildings, cobblestone lanes, and a variety of interesting stores and restaurants, provides tourists a look into the island's legendary history. Join us as we go back in time to visit the lovely Historic Downtown Fernandina Beach.

The Heart of Downtown: Centre Street:

The busy core of Historic Downtown Fernandina Beach is Centre Street. This lively street is dotted with an eclectic mix of shops, art galleries, antique stores, and restaurants.

Take a leisurely walk through the brick-paved streets and marvel at the well-preserved buildings from the late nineteenth and early twentieth century. The Victorian structures, with their elegant facades and ornamental features, bear witness to the area's rich past.

Amelia Island History Museum:

The Amelia Island Museum of History, located on South 3rd Street, is a must-see for history buffs. The museum, housed in the historic Nassau County Jail, has exhibits covering the island's history, including Native American beginnings, Spanish colonization, the Golden Age of Pirates, and the Gilded Age. Displays, antiques, and interactive aspects help visitors comprehend the island's unique cultural background.

Landmarks and historic churches:

Historic Downtown Fernandina Beach is peppered with attractive churches and monuments, all of which contribute to the area's architectural beauty. The Nassau County Courthouse, an enormous red-brick structure that serves as a vivid reminder of the island's judicial history, is one of the famous monuments.

St. Michael's Catholic Church, Florida's oldest Catholic parish, and the United Methodist Church of Fernandina Beach are additional noteworthy historic sites worth seeing.

The Palace Saloon is the oldest bar in Florida:

The Palace Saloon is a must-see for anybody visiting Historic Downtown Fernandina Beach. The Palace Saloon is Florida's oldest saloon, having been founded in 1903. Step inside and you'll be taken back in time thanks to the old wooden bar, tin ceiling, and historical pictures adorning the walls. Enjoy a cool drink while taking in the vibrant ambiance of this historic institution.

Fernandina Beach Market:

Don't miss the Fernandina Beach Market Place if you're in town on a Saturday morning. This lively farmers market on North 7th Street offers a delectable selection of locally produced fruit, handmade crafts, artisanal delights, and live entertainment. Experience the essence of the town by interacting with local sellers and discovering unique artifacts to take home as mementos.

Walking Tours of the Historic District:

Consider taking a guided walking tour of the Historic District to thoroughly immerse yourself in the area's history and architecture. Several tour companies give informative guided tours with intriguing tales, stories, and lesser-known facts about the structures and people that created the town's past.

Historic Downtown Fernandina Beach is a quaint and intriguing location that takes tourists back in time. The neighborhood provides a beautiful combination of history, culture, and local character, with its well-preserved architecture, intriguing museums, and thriving retail and eating scene.

Whether wandering along Centre Street, seeing the Amelia Island Museum of History, or soaking in the atmosphere of the Palace Saloon, a visit to Historic Downtown Fernandina Beach is a trip back in time that will leave an indelible impression.

History Museum

The Amelia Island Museum of History is a cultural jewel that invites visitors to dive into Amelia Island's and the surrounding region's fascinating history. This museum, located in the center of Fernandina Beach, Florida, provides a full and immersive experience that highlights the island's rich past, different cultures, and significant historical milestones.

Join us as we travel through time and discover the intriguing exhibits and tales housed at the Amelia Island Museum of History.

History Of The Museum:

The museum offers an enthralling look into Amelia Island's Native American heritage, which date back thousands of years.

Visitors receive insight into the island's early inhabitants, their way of life, and their ongoing legacy via exhibitions, antiques, and interactive displays. Discover the Timucua people's tales and their intimate relationship to the island's natural surroundings.

Beyond Spanish Colonization:

Explore exhibits that shed light on Amelia Island's importance during this important time as you step into the age of Spanish exploration and colonization.

Learn about Spanish missions, European settlement, and the island's strategic significance throughout the colonial period. Exhibits and historical relics provide insight into the Spanish influence that impacted the island's early history.

Amelia Island Pirates:

Discover the enthralling stories of pirates that once roamed the seas around Amelia Island. Learn about the island's ties to notable pirates including the infamous French pirate Louis-Michel Aury and the famed pirate queen Anne Bonny. Exhibits bring the Golden Age of Piracy to life, with antiques, interactive displays, and enthralling tales of adventure on the high seas.

The Golden Age:

The museum also provides a glimpse into the affluent Gilded Age, an era of affluence and splendor in the late nineteenth and early twentieth century. Discover the charm of the island's Victorian-period houses, the railroad's effect on the island's growth, and the bustling social scene that thrived during this era. Explore exhibits that show the island's economic development, the emergence of tourism, and the prominent personalities who left their imprint on Amelia Island.

Local History & Community Stories:

The Amelia Island Museum of History honors the island's unique cultural past as well as the tales of its residents. The museum illuminates the experiences of ordinary people who have molded the island's character via oral histories, personal tales, and community partnerships. Learn more about the island's varied fabric, including the contributions of African Americans, immigrants, and other ethnic groups that have called Amelia Island home.

Exhibits and Events of Note:

The museum hosts unique exhibitions on a regular basis that focus on different areas of Amelia Island's history, culture, and art. These temporary displays give a new viewpoint and opportunity to learn more about the island's history. Throughout the year, the museum also conducts a range of events, lectures, and workshops that provide further insights into the island's history and promote a greater understanding for its unique cultural tapestry.

The Amelia Island Museum of History provides an enthralling window into the island's rich history. The museum brings to life the varied cultures, key historical events, and interesting characters that have defined Amelia Island's identity via engaging exhibits, interactive displays, and thought-provoking storytelling.

A visit to this extraordinary museum is a voyage through time, giving visitors with a deep grasp of the island's origins and a lasting admiration for its rich and legendary past.

Cumberland Island National Seashore

Cumberland Island National Seashore, a hidden jewel off Georgia's coast, provides an enticing getaway into unspoilt natural beauty and interesting history.

This remote barrier island welcomes travelers seeking an amazing and awe-inspiring experience with its beautiful beaches, old oak woods, and historic ruins. Join us on an enthralling adventure across Cumberland Island National Seashore, where nature and history collide to create an amazing coastal paradise.

Beautiful Beaches:

Cumberland Island has nearly 17 kilometers of pristine sandy beaches that go along the Atlantic Ocean. Take leisurely stroll down the beach, dip your toes in the soft sand, and soak in the peace and quiet of these unspoiled coastal beauties. Witness the rhythmic dance of the waves, hunt for seashells and sand dollars, and enjoy the peace that these remote beaches provide.

Natural Beauty and the Wilderness:

Cumberland Island, designated as a National Seashore, is a refuge for nature lovers and outdoor enthusiasts. Explore the natural wildness of the island, which includes maritime forests, tidal marshes, and vast salt marsh ecosystems. Immerse yourself in the island's different ecosystems and meet a variety of animals, including wild horses, armadillos, deer, and a variety of bird species. Keep a look out for the island's famous stray horses, which will give a magical touch to your tour.

Ruins of Dungeness:

The eerily stunning Dungeness Ruins are located in the middle of Cumberland Island. This ancient home, formerly the great residence of the Carnegie family, today stands as a captivating testimony to the island's historical history. Explore the mansion's ruins, roam around its overgrown grounds, and let your imagination take you to another time. The remains provide a peek into the island's former splendor and intrigue.

Nature and hiking trails:

Cumberland Island has an extensive network of paths that weave across its pristine landscapes, providing exceptional exploring possibilities. Whether you follow the picturesque South End Loop route through maritime woods and to breathtaking coastline vistas, or the shady tranquillity of the Willow Pond Trail, each route shows a different aspect of the island's natural beauty. Explore the tranquillity of the island as you walk beneath old oak canopies, through dunes, and across marshes.

Nesting of sea turtles:

Cumberland Island is critical to the survival of sea turtles, particularly the endangered loggerhead turtle. If you come during the nesting season (May to October), you could be lucky enough to see mother turtles depositing their eggs or hatchlings making their journey to the ocean. Witnessing this natural beauty is an awe-inspiring experience that serves as a reminder of the island's dedication to conserving its valuable species.

Overnight Camping and Stays:

Consider camping overnight on Cumberland Island for a more immersive experience. The coastline has designated campsites where you may pitch a tent and spend the night among the wild beauty of the island. Awakening to the soft rustle of leaves and falling asleep to the sound of waves breaking on the coast is an excellent opportunity to connect with nature and build lifelong memories.

Cumberland Island National Seashore is an enthralling combination of untainted wildness, rich history, and magnificent coastline scenery. This coastal paradise provides a one-of-a-kind and spectacular experience, from its beautiful beaches and old woods to its eerie ruins and plentiful animals. Exploring Cumberland Island National Seashore enables you to immerse yourself in nature's beauties, experience a feeling of calm, and connect with a place where the untold stories of the past are told.

Egans Creek Greenway

Egans Creek Greenway is a hidden refuge of natural beauty and quiet on Amelia Island, Florida. This enthralling preserve, which includes different ecosystems and picturesque pathways, provides visitors with a tranquil haven where they can immerse themselves in the island's natural surroundings. Join us on an enthralling adventure through Egans Creek Greenway, where natural delights await at every turn.

Scenic Walkways and Nature Trails:

The Egans Creek Greenway is a network of well-kept natural paths and picturesque walkways that travel through a range of enthralling surroundings. Take in the sights and sounds of nature as you stroll along the shady walkways surrounded by lush flora and towering oak trees. The pathways provide an immersive experience inside this natural refuge, allowing for leisurely walks, exciting treks, and animal viewing.

Salt Marshes and Wetlands:

You'll pass through lovely wetlands and salt marshes brimming with life as you walk the Egans Creek Greenway. Admire the brilliant green colors of the marsh grasses, listen to the cacophony of singing birds, and see wading herons and beautiful egrets.

Wetlands offer critical habitat for a wide range of animals, including turtles, fish, and various bird species, resulting in an enthralling environment to explore.

Birdwatching and Wildlife Observation:

The Egans Creek Greenway is a paradise for birdwatchers and wildlife enthusiasts alike. Bring your binoculars and be prepared to see a wide variety of avian species such as roseate spoonbills, ibises, ospreys, and red-winged blackbirds. The quiet environment and vast natural resources attract a plethora of species, providing extraordinary opportunity to watch and engage with nature's delicate balance.

Rest Stops and Picnic Areas:
There are appealing picnic spots and rest stations along the Egans Creek Greenway, giving the ideal place to halt, relax, and enjoy a pleasant outdoor meal among nature's calm. Relax on a shady seat, enjoy the cool air, and take in the beauty that surrounds you. These designated areas provide an excellent chance to refresh and enjoy the calm environment of the greenway.

Interpretive and educational signage:
The Egans Creek Greenway is both a picturesque and educational resource. Along the paths, you'll come across interesting signs and interpretive stations that will teach you about the area flora, wildlife, and ecological processes. These educational components enhance your experience by generating a greater knowledge and respect for the natural beauties that flourish along the greenway.

Conservation and preservation of the environment:

The Egans Creek Greenway is a remarkable example of environmental and land preservation initiatives. The greenway is critical to the preservation of the island's natural resources, including wetlands, animal habitats, and water quality. Take a time to think on the importance of maintaining these natural areas for future generations to enjoy as you explore this tranquil refuges.

The Egans Creek Greenway provides a peaceful getaway into the natural splendor of Amelia Island's surroundings. This greenway gives a reprieve from the stresses of daily life, with its meandering nature paths and intriguing wetlands, as well as its plentiful animals and tranquil picnic sites.

Exploring Egans Creek Greenway enables you to reconnect with nature, find peace in its peacefulness, and get a new respect for the fragile ecosystems that make Amelia Island such a special place.

CHAPTER THREE

AMELIA ISLAND'S TOP RESTAURANTS AND EATERIES

Traditional Amelia Island Restaurant

Amelia Island is well-known not just for its beautiful beaches and historical significance, but also for its diversified food scene. Traditional Amelia Island restaurants stand out among the variety of eating alternatives, giving a lovely combination of tastes, friendly hospitality, and a sense of the island's culinary history.

Join us on a delightful trip into the heart of traditional Amelia Island dining, where tasty food and attractive ambience combine to create a memorable experience.

Delights in Fresh Seafood:

It's no wonder that fish takes center stage at traditional Amelia Island restaurants, given the island's seaside position. Savor fresh catch-of-the-day meals, juicy shrimp, delicious crab cakes, and tempting oysters as you indulge in the bounty of the Atlantic Ocean.

These restaurants, ranging from simple fish shacks to upscale seafood places, provide a delicious selection of seafood specialties, providing a memorable gastronomic trip for seafood fans.

Southern Comfort Cuisine:

Traditional Amelia Island restaurants reflect the American South's rich culinary heritage, serving a variety of soothing and soulful cuisine. These eateries capture the heart of Southern hospitality on every dish, from delicate barbecue ribs and fried chicken to traditional collard greens, cornbread, and creamy macaroni and cheese. Enjoy the flavors that have made Southern food famous for its heartiness and down-home charm.

Sea Inspired Cuisine:

The seaside backdrop of Amelia Island generates a unique blend of tastes in traditional eateries. Dishes that combine seafood, fresh vegetables, and regional flavors are available.

Enjoy local delicacies in meals like shrimp and grits, she-crab soup, low-country boils, and grilled grouper. These culinary masterpieces honor the island's coastal history, infusing each taste with a touch of marine charm.

Farm-to-Table Dishes:

Traditional Amelia Island restaurants embrace the farm-to-table movement, highlighting the island's agricultural wealth and supporting local farmers. Chefs convert the freshness and tastes of locally obtained foods into artistic and appetizing meals.

These restaurants reflect the region's sustainable and thriving culinary culture, serving everything from fresh vegetables to grass-fed meats and artisanal cheeses.

Historic settings and a charming atmosphere:

Traditional Amelia Island restaurants are distinguished by their intriguing surroundings, which are often situated inside ancient houses that emit a certain charm.

Dine in restored Victorian-era décor, lovely patios, or warm interiors that take you back in time. These restaurants' warm and friendly environment adds an added layer of charm, delivering a remarkable dining experience that mixes history, culture, and gastronomic enjoyment.

Local Hospitality & Complimentary Service:

The authentic warmth and kindness of the island's restaurant personnel completes the classic Amelia Island dining experience. You'll be welcomed with welcoming smiles and attentive care the minute you walk through the door. The staff's genuine love of local food and dedication to providing a wonderful dining experience guarantees that every visitor feels welcomed and departs with a pleased smile.

Traditional Amelia Island restaurants provide a gastronomic adventure that celebrates the island's coastal beauty, Southern history, and farm-to-table philosophy. These restaurants exhibit the region's unique cuisines and culinary traditions, from fresh marine specialties to comfortable Southern favorites.

Dining at a typical Amelia Island restaurant is not only a delicious culinary experience but also a celebration of the island's cultural past, thanks to historic settings, attractive ambience, and genuine hospitality. Set out on a savory excursion and let Amelia Island's traditional food make a lasting effect on your taste buds and heart.

Amelia Island International Cuisine Restaurants

Amelia Island is a mesmerizing resort with gorgeous beaches and a rich history, as well as a dynamic culinary scene that spans the world. You'll find a broad selection of ethnic cuisine restaurants on the island's quaint streets, each presenting a delightful voyage of tastes and culinary traditions. Join us on a worldwide culinary excursion as we explore the ethnic tastes found on the menus of Amelia Island's foreign cuisine restaurants.

Delights from the Mediterranean:

At Amelia Island's foreign cuisine restaurants, savor the tastes of the Mediterranean. Taste the zesty tastes of Greek cuisine with meals like moussaka, souvlaki, and spanakopita.

With handcrafted pasta, wood-fired pizzas, and creamy tiramisu, you may indulge in the rich tastes of Italian food. Whether you're seeking the fresh ingredients of a Greek salad or the rich tastes of a Mediterranean seafood stew, these eateries on the island provide a true sense of the Mediterranean.

Fusion Asian Cuisine:

Without leaving Amelia Island, go on a gastronomic tour around Asia. Asian fusion restaurants mix the finest of diverse Asian cuisines to create a flavor explosion that will tickle your taste buds. Enjoy Thai cuisine's vivid spices, the delicate tastes of sushi and sashimi, or the savory pleasures of Chinese stir-fries. These eateries deliver the variety and lively tastes of Asia to your plate, from Thai curries to Japanese ramen and Vietnamese pho.

Latin American Influence:

At Amelia Island's world cuisine restaurants, you may immerse yourself in the rich and colorful culinary traditions of Latin America. With scorching fajitas, tangy ceviche, and savory enchiladas, indulge in the robust and hot tastes of Mexican food. Ceviche, lomo saltado, and causa are just a few of the flavorful and varied Peruvian meals to try. These eateries give a taste of Latin America on the island, whether you're looking for fiery Mexican street tacos or the soothing tastes of Cuban food.

Culinary Fusions and International Fusions:

Amelia Island's world cuisine restaurants also practice culinary fusion, combining tastes from several locations to produce unique and intriguing meals. Explore the harmonic blending of tastes from throughout the globe, such as when Thai meets French or Latin American spices meet Caribbean influences. These ingenious and imaginative culinary concoctions provide a one-of-a-kind dining experience that highlights the island's chefs' different abilities and culinary expertise.

Wine & Beverage Selections from Around the World:

A carefully chosen assortment of world wines and drinks will complement your international culinary experience. Many Amelia Island ethnic cuisine restaurants have a comprehensive wine selection that includes vintages from world-renowned wine areas. Enhance your dining experience by pairing precisely matched wines, handmade cocktails, or specialty drinks with each cuisine's culture and customs.

Cultural Ambience and Real-Life Experiences:

Aside from the delectable tastes, the world cuisine restaurants on Amelia Island often reproduce the cultural ambience and eating experiences associated with their unique cuisines. These restaurants attempt to offer an authentic dining experience that conveys you to the heart of each culinary culture, from vivid décor and traditional music to attentive service and informed personnel.

Amelia Island's diverse cuisine restaurants provide a passport to the world's delicacies. From fragrant Asian spices to tempting Mediterranean tastes, Latin American flare, and inventive culinary fusions, these restaurants showcase the island's eclectic gastronomic scene. Set out on a worldwide gastronomic trip and let Amelia Island's foreign cuisine restaurants take you to other countries via the art of culinary excellence and cultural immersion.

Indulge your senses and expand your gastronomic horizons.

Cafes and Restaurants in Amelia Island

Amelia Island is a culinary wonderland, with a bustling and diversified culinary culture that appeals to all tastes. The island offers a fascinating choice of eating alternatives, ranging from modest cafés selling scrumptious pastries and artisanal coffees to famous restaurants presenting a combination of tastes and culinary expertise.

Join us on a gastronomic adventure as we explore the delectable tastes and attractive ambience of Amelia Island's cafés and eateries.

Bakeries and cafés:

Begin your day by visiting one of Amelia Island's charming cafés and bakeries, where the fragrance of freshly brewed coffee and baked delicacies fills the air.

Along with your expertly made cup of coffee or espresso, indulge in flaky croissants, buttery pastries, and luscious sweets. These cafés provide a warm and scented start to your day, whether you're looking for a quiet spot to enjoy a leisurely breakfast or a quick pick-me-up on the run.

Coastal and Seafood Cuisine:

Amelia Island, being a seaside resort, has an abundance of seafood-focused eateries that highlight the region's marine history. Succulent shrimp, melt-in-your-mouth grouper, and buttery lobster served in a variety of delectable methods are available.

Whether you choose a modest seafood shack or an expensive waterfront restaurant, these eateries showcase the freshest fish and allow you to experience the aromas of the sea.

Soul Food and Southern Comfort:

At Amelia Island's Southern comfort food restaurants, embrace Southern hospitality and indulge in soulful meals.

These eateries feature big amounts of comfort cuisine that will fulfill every appetite, from crunchy fried chicken and smokey barbecue ribs to creamy macaroni & cheese and collard greens. You'll feel right at home in the warm and friendly ambiance if you pair your meal with a side of Southern hospitality.

Flavors from Around the World:

The culinary culture on Amelia Island draws influence from all around the globe, with restaurants serving a variety of ethnic cuisines.

Discover the delectable tastes of Italian, Mexican, Asian, and Mediterranean cuisines. Authentic pasta meals, spicy tacos, aromatic curries, and delectable kebabs are all masterfully cooked using traditional ingredients and methods. Without leaving the island, you may go on a worldwide gastronomic trip at these foreign eateries.

Excellence in Farm-to-Table Cuisine:

Amelia Island's farm-to-table restaurants provide the finest of the island's local fruit, meats, and artisanal products to guests looking for a farm-fresh eating experience.

These restaurants showcase the region's strong agricultural legacy by serving everything from farm-fresh salads and organic vegetables to grass-fed meats and sustainable seafood. Enjoy seasonal delicacies while supporting local producers and adopting a sustainable eating philosophy.

Culinary Excellence and Fine Dining:

Amelia Island also has a number of upmarket restaurants that provide amazing culinary offerings as well as great service. Fine dining at its finest, where exceptional chefs display their skills via meticulously created tasting menus and culinary wonders.

These restaurants have a classy environment, comprehensive wine lists, and a dedication to offering an extraordinary dining experience that will satisfy even the most discriminating palates.

The cafés and restaurants on Amelia Island provide a delicious blend of tastes, culinary traditions, and a friendly ambience. The island's culinary sector caters to all tastes and inclinations, with everything from quiet cafés offering delightful pastries to seafood-focused enterprises, foreign cuisines, farm-to-table experiences, and fine dining places. Amelia Island's cafés and restaurants are likely to make a lasting impact on your taste buds and create treasured culinary memories, whether you're looking for a fast coffee fix, a casual lunch with friends, or an amazing culinary experience.

CHAPTER FOUR

AMELIA NIGHTLIFE EXPERIENCE

Amelia Island's Vibrant Night Bars and Nightclubs

When the sun goes down on Amelia Island, the colorful nightlife comes alive, allowing tourists and residents alike to relax, interact, and dance the night away. Amelia Island's nightlife culture offers something for everyone, from bustling pubs selling specialty drinks and local breweries to frenetic nightclubs pulsing with music and excitement.

Join us as we explore the electric world of Amelia Island's pubs and nightclubs, where amazing experiences and treasured memories await.

The Palace Saloon:

The Palace Saloon, known as Florida's oldest saloon, has been a popular drinking establishment since 1903. With its original oak bar, tin ceiling, and old portraits lining the walls, this renowned tavern transports you back in time. Enjoy a broad variety of specialty beers, artisan drinks, and live music filling the air. The vibrant ambiance and rich history of the Palace Saloon make it a must-visit site for anyone looking for a taste of Amelia Island's past and present.

Green Turtle Tavern:

14 South 3rd Street, Fernandina Beach

The Green Turtle Tavern, located in the center of downtown Fernandina Beach, provides a relaxed and inviting ambiance. This neighborhood favorite is known for its friendly staff and wide drink menu, which includes traditional cocktails, specialty beers, and unique shots. Join in on the fun with live music, karaoke nights, and vibrant discussions that make every visit to The Green Turtle Tavern special.

Salty Pelican Bar and Grill:

Fernandina Beach's address is 12 N Front St.

The Salty Pelican Bar & Grill, located along the beachfront in Fernandina Beach, mixes superb cuisine with a lively bar atmosphere. While sipping handmade drinks, take in the breathtaking views of the marina. The bar offers a comprehensive range of craft beers, wines, and specialty cocktails, as well as a menu of delectable seafood, burgers, and other pub fare. The vibrant mood and gorgeous environment of The Salty Pelican make for a great night out.

The Dog Star Tavern:
Fernandina Beach's address is 10 N 2nd St.

Dog Star Tavern is a must-see place for music fans. This tiny live music venue showcases both local and visiting musicians, with styles ranging from rock to blues to reggae. While enjoying your favorite beer or beverage, take in the colorful ambiance and dance to the beat of the music. Dog Star Tavern's dedication to local performers and offering a great live music experience distinguishes it as a fixture of Amelia Island's nightlife.

The Patio Location:
416 Ash Street, Fernandina Beach

The Patio Place, known for its bright outside patio, is a bustling pub where residents and tourists alike gather to enjoy a laid-back ambiance and delicious cocktails. Sip on inventive cocktails, artisan brews, or pick from a wide wine list. The courteous staff and warm atmosphere of the pub make it a popular destination for mingling and making new acquaintances. The Patio location will not disappoint whether you're searching for a relaxing evening with friends or a location to start your night out.

The pubs and nightclubs on Amelia Island provide an exhilarating nightlife experience that appeals to a wide range of interests and inclinations. These locations provide remarkable experiences and possibilities to make treasured memories, ranging from old saloons steeped in history to contemporary businesses pulsing with music and excitement.

So, whether you're looking for specialty drinks, live music, waterfront views, or a bustling dance floor, Amelia Island's bars and nightclubs are eager to bring the nightlife to you.

Amelia Island Live Music Centres

Amelia Island is not just a gorgeous coastal beauty, but it is also a live music hotspot, with the lovely sounds of great artists filling the air and creating a memorable environment.

The island's live music venues range from small settings that highlight local talent to bigger venues that draw famous musicians. Join us on a melodious tour around Amelia Island's enthralling live music scene, where music becomes inextricably linked to the island's dynamic culture.

Amelia Island's Ritz-Carlton:

Fernandina Beach, 4750 Amelia Island Pkwy

The Ritz-Carlton, Amelia Island is an opulent facility that delivers great live music events in a polished and beautiful atmosphere. Experience the enchantment of live music in one of the resort's elegant bars or outdoor locations, where famous artists captivate audiences with their exceptional skill. The Ritz-Carlton provides an appealing ambience that improves the live music experience, from peaceful jazz to vibrant piano performances.

The Dog Star Tavern:

Fernandina Beach's address is 10 N 2nd St.

Dog Star Tavern is a hidden treasure on Amelia Island that delivers the energy of live music. This compact and varied venue features local and traveling musicians from a variety of genres such as rock, blues, reggae, and more.

Immerse yourself in the exciting environment, make new friends, and let the pulse of the music spark your spirit. Dog Star Tavern's dedication to promoting local musicians and offering a genuine live music experience has earned it a place in the hearts of both artists and music fans.

Amelia Island Coffee:

207 Centre Street, Fernandina Beach

Amelia Island Coffee mixes the welcoming atmosphere of a café with the appeal of live music. This quaint and pleasant location features live performances on a regular basis, enabling customers to drink their favorite coffee or beverage while listening to the calming sounds of local performers.

Amelia Island Coffee produces an intimate and easygoing setting that develops a true connection between the performers and the audience, from acoustic concerts to intimate singer-songwriter performances.

The Green Turtle Tavern:

14 South 3rd Street, Fernandina Beach

The Green Turtle Tavern is not just a vibrant tavern, but it is also a live music hotspot on Amelia Island. This local favorite has a pleasant and inviting ambience and showcases excellent performers who fill the air with intriguing sounds.

The Green Turtle Tavern offers a welcoming place for both local talent and visiting performers, whether it's acoustic concerts, lively bands, or intriguing open mic evenings. Join the crowd, sip your favorite beverage, and let the music take you away.

Amelia River Golf:

Amelia Island's address is 4477 Buccaneer Trail.

Amelia River Golf Club is well-known not just for its golfing experience, but also for its live music events on its stunning outdoor stage. This picturesque location is ideal for enjoying live music against a background of lush nature and calm surroundings. The Amelia River Golf Club offers a unique and unforgettable outdoor live music experience that mixes natural beauty with compelling melodies, from local bands to traveling performers.

The live music venues on Amelia Island provide a compelling and musical trip that adds to the island's diverse cultural fabric. From The Ritz-Carlton's refined ambiance to the intimate settings of Dog Star Tavern, Amelia Island Coffee, the Green Turtle Tavern, and the Amelia River Golf Club, each venue offers a one-of-a-kind space for talented musicians to showcase their artistry and create unforgettable experiences for the audience.

So, whether you're looking for soul-stirring tunes or a bustling setting to dance the night away, Amelia Island's live music venues offer to fill your nights with fun and entertainment.

Amelia Island's Theaters & Performances

Amelia Island is not only a natural beauty refuge, but it is also a cultural hub with a strong theater and performing arts industry. The island provides a broad range of theatrical experiences, from old theaters showing classic plays to contemporary venues featuring a variety of shows.

Join us as we discover Amelia Island's magnificent world of theaters and plays, where imagination, skill, and engaging narrative take center stage.

Amelia Community Theatre presents:

209 Cedar Street, Fernandina Beach

The Amelia Community Theatre is a cultural landmark on the island, presenting a diverse variety of theatrical events. The community theater captivates spectators with its superb performances, which range from classic dramas and comedies to current works and musicals.

Step inside the beautifully refurbished arena and you'll be taken to a world of intriguing narrative and the transforming power of live theater.

Bistro at Story & Song Bookstore:

Fernandina Beach's address is 1430 Park Ave.

While Story & Song is best known as a bookshop and café, it also provides a unique location for private performances and creative expressions.

This intimate facility presents a range of activities, such as live music concerts, poetry readings, and author engagements. In this inviting and creative setting, enjoy an evening of captivating tunes or thought-provoking literary conversations while eating a wonderful meal or a cup of coffee.

Amelia Musical Playhouse:

Fernandina Beach's 1955 Island Walkway

Amelia Musical Playhouse is an island treasure committed to fostering and presenting the abilities of local artists. This community theater puts on musical shows in a variety of genres and styles to appeal to a wide spectrum of viewers. The Amelia Musical Playhouse provides a unique and entertaining theatrical experience for both the artists and the audience, ranging from Broadway blockbusters to original creations.

Festivals:

Throughout the year, Amelia Island also hosts a number of festivals and events that promote the performing arts. The Amelia Island

Jazz Festival features world-class jazz performers that delight audiences with heartfelt melodies and engaging improvisation.

The Amelia Island Chamber Music Festival features world-class chamber musicians, whilst the Amelia Island Theatre Festival has a broad schedule of theatrical acts such as comedies, dramas, and experimental pieces. These events allow chances to immerse yourself in Amelia Island's unique tapestry of performing arts.

Performances in School and in the Community:

The robust theatrical industry on Amelia Island goes beyond specific theaters, with performances taking place in schools and community centers. Local schools and groups often create performances that showcase young performers' skills, demonstrating their originality and love for the performing arts. These community concerts promote solidarity and provide budding performers a chance to shine, adding to the island's unique cultural tapestry.

The theaters and shows on Amelia Island provide a thrilling and beautiful world of creativity and creative expression. From professional plays at Amelia Community Theatre to small performances at Story & Song Bookstore Bistro and community-driven acts at Amelia Musical

Playhouse, the island's theaters provide a chance to be immersed in the transformational power of live performances.

Whether you're a theater enthusiast or just looking for a night of entertainment, Amelia Island's theaters and shows will pique your interest and leave you with a great respect for the arts.

CHAPTER FIVE

SHOPPING IN AMELIA ISLAND

Amelia Island Gifts and Souvenirs

With its rich history and lively culture, Amelia Island provides a treasure trove of one-of-a-kind gifts and souvenirs for tourists to take home and remember. Whether you're looking for a souvenir to remember your vacation or a unique present for a loved one, the island's lovely stores and boutiques are full of fascinating bargains.

Join us on a mesmerizing voyage as we explore the world of Amelia Island gifts & souvenirs, where you may uncover treasures that encapsulate the spirit of this enchanting place.

Nautical and Seashell Treasures:

Amelia Island, being an island attraction, has an abundance of seashells and nautical-themed goods. Explore local stores and boutiques for a gorgeous array of seashells, starfish, and one-of-a-kind beachcombing items.

Choose finely carved seashell jewelry, ornamental items, or framed seashell art to take home a piece of the island's coastline. These gems not only bring back memories of your beach trips, but they also honor the island's coastal character.

Handmade Artwork and Crafts:

Amelia Island has a thriving arts culture, and visiting the island's native artwork and crafts is a lovely opportunity to immerse yourself in the creative spirit. Visit galleries and artisan stores where you may see the work of local painters, sculptors, potters, and craftspeople. Paintings, pottery, jewelry, woodwork, and textiles are among the artisan things available. These one-of-a-kind items exhibit the island's creative skill in a meaningful and unique way.

Gourmet Delights & Culinary Memorabilia:

The food culture on Amelia Island is a veritable treasure trove of gastronomic treats, and what better way to record the island's tastes than via gourmet souvenirs? Discover specialized food shops and culinary businesses that sell handmade jams, jellies, sauces, spices, and chocolates. Indulge in the island's culinary legacy by choosing distinctive flavors that bring the taste of Amelia Island to your own kitchen, or treat friends and family back home with a delectable edible memento of your trip.

Keepsakes from the Past:

The rich history of Amelia Island is strongly embedded in its culture, and there are various stores selling vintage souvenirs and artifacts. Browse antique stores and specialized shops for historic maps, postcards, pictures, and publications that provide insight into the island's history. Replicas of historic antiques, historic-inspired jewelry, or even locally created items that combine parts of the island's tradition are examples of distinctive historic mementos.

Spa and Wellness Items:

Amelia Island is associated with relaxation and renewal, and what better way to bring some of that peace and quiet into your house than with spa and health products?

Find handcrafted soaps, luxury bath salts, aromatherapy oils, and skincare items prepared with natural ingredients inspired by the island's flora in local stores. These items not only give a relaxing and delicious experience, but they also serve as a daily reminder of the island's tranquil atmosphere.

Apparel and Accessories Inspired by the Islands:

Choose trendy garments and accessories that express the atmosphere of Amelia Island to embrace the island's laid-back appeal. Explore businesses that sell island-inspired items, such as colorful beachwear, airy dresses, and comfy t-shirts with local motifs. Accessorize your style with hats, sunglasses, and jewelry that showcase maritime themes or the island's distinctive flora and wildlife.

The gift and souvenir stores on Amelia Island are a treasure trove of one-of-a-kind items that represent the island's natural beauty, lively culture, and rich history. From seashell treasures and locally crafted artwork to gourmet foods, there's something for everyone.

Walking and Biking Tours
For Tourist

With its stunning surroundings and rich history, Amelia Island is best visited at a leisurely pace, enabling visitors to completely immerse themselves in its compelling attractions. Walking and bike trips are ideal for discovering the island's hidden secrets, which range from historic places to breathtaking views and pleasant communities.

Join us on an enthralling adventure across Amelia Island's tourist sites through energizing walking and bicycling excursions, where every stride and pedal stroke exposes the island's fascination.

Tour of Historic Downtown Fernandina Beach:

Take a walking tour of downtown Fernandina Beach's historic streets, where the island's rich past comes to life. As you travel along Centre Street, take in the magnificent Victorian buildings, quaint boutiques, and delightful eateries.

Visit the Old Nassau County Courthouse, the Palace Saloon, and the Amelia Island Museum of History, among other historic sites. Allow the stories of pirates, shrimpers, and railroad tycoons to unravel as you learn about the intriguing people who influenced the island's history.

Trail Biking Adventure on Amelia Island:

Set off on a bike ride down the Amelia Island Trail, a gorgeous trail that runs the whole length of the island. Rent a bike and ride across the gorgeous coastal vistas, maritime woods, and lovely wetlands.

As you ride through scenic beaches and get sights of the island's plentiful wildlife, enjoy the invigorating ocean wind. This bicycling trip enables you to immerse yourself in the natural beauty of the island while having an exhilarating outdoor experience.

Exploration of Fort Clinch State Park:

Explore the historic Fort Clinch State Park, a reconstructed Civil War-era stronghold situated in magnificent natural surroundings. Explore the fort's unique architecture, take in the stunning views of Cumberland Sound, and walk the park's nature paths.

Guided tours of the fort's interesting history are available, as are historical reenactments that bring the past to life. This walking tour offers a one-of-a-kind combination of history, wildlife, and natural splendor.

Beachcombing and shell collecting:

The beautiful beaches of Amelia Island provide a magnificent background for a pleasant and enriching walking trip. Remove your shoes and feel the sand between your toes as you walk around the beach in search of seashells and beach treasures.

Discover the marine species that washes ashore while learning about the island's coastal environment. Allow the rhythm of the waves and the tranquility of the surroundings to create a pleasant and wonderful experience as you explore the island's beaches.

Egans Creek Greenway Nature Walk:

A calm nature stroll via Egans Creek Greenway will immerse you in the island's natural splendor. This protected sanctuary has tranquil walking routes that travel through a variety of environments, including wetlands, salt marshes, and oak-lined walkways.

Observe the island's abundant birds, spot animals, and take in the sounds of nature. This walking trip allows you to reconnect with the natural environment of the island and admire its biological beauty.

Trail at Amelia Island Plantation Nature Center:

A guided walking tour of Amelia Island's natural marvels is available at the Amelia Island

Plantation Nature Center. Explore the beautiful maritime forest, stroll along shady pathways, and hear from experienced guides about the island's flora and animals.

Discover rare plant species, witness natural fauna, and gaze out over the marshes and rivers. This walking tour provides a peaceful and informative experience in the center of the island's natural splendor.

Walking and bike excursions on Amelia Island provide intriguing and immersive experiences, enabling visitors to discover the island's charm one step at a time.

Amelia Island Summer Activities

During the summer months, Amelia Island comes alive with exciting events and wonderful experiences for guests of all ages. The island is a summer adventurer's dream, with everything from sun-kissed beaches and exhilarating water sports to interesting wildlife discoveries and cultural activities. Join us as we explore the enthralling world of summer activities on Amelia Island, where the opportunities are limitless and the memories are priceless.

Beach Relaxation and Water Sports:

The gorgeous beaches of Amelia Island are a haven for sunbathers and water sports lovers. Bask in the warm embrace of the sun on sandy beaches, take soothing dives in the glistening sea, and create sandcastles with your loved ones. For those looking for more daring activities, consider adrenaline water sports like paddleboarding, kayaking, jet skiing, or surfing. Snorkel the island's unique marine life or take a leisurely boat cruise to see dolphins and admire the stunning coastline vistas.

Nature Explorations and Eco-Tours:

Immerse yourself in the natural splendor of the island with eco-tours and environmental expeditions that reveal the island's different ecosystems. Take guided kayak trips along quiet rivers to see a diverse range of bird species, explore wetlands, and learn about the island's endangered environment. Take a sunset sail along the Amelia River to see the splendor of the golden hour as the wildlife comes to life. Discover the island's rich marine woods and pathways, which are ideal for hiking and bicycling and provide views of the island's flora and animals.

Golfing Prowess:
Amelia Island is a golfer's dream, with beautiful courses offering breathtaking vistas and tough fairways. Tee off at one of the island's top golf courses, which have perfectly groomed greens set by stunning scenery. Experience championship-level golf while relaxing in the island's tranquil setting, surrounded by nature's splendor. Amelia Island's golfing expertise offers a wonderful experience, whether you're a seasoned golfer or a newbie wishing to try your hand at the sport.

Cultural Festivals and Events:
Summer on Amelia Island delivers a plethora of festivals and cultural events that highlight the island's rich past and lively vibe. The Amelia Island Chamber Music Festival features world-class artists who fascinate listeners with their skill. The annual Isle of Eight Flags Shrimp Festival honors the island's nautical past with live music, arts and crafts merchants, and delectable seafood. Participate in art walks, farmers markets, and outdoor concerts, all of which provide a diverse tapestry of cultural experiences.

Culinary & Dining Adventures:
Summer is the ideal season to sample the island's gastronomic offerings and enjoy al fresco dining

at its finest. Explore the island's eclectic restaurant scene, which includes everything from informal seafood shacks to luxury dining venues where fresh catch-of-the-day and farm-to-table products take center stage. Savor tasty cuisine that highlight the island's coastal tastes and cosmopolitan influences over a romantic sunset supper on the waterfront. Treat your taste buds to delectable gastronomic excursions and appreciate the culinary gems of the island.

Wellness and relaxation:

Amelia Island provides an exquisite place for refreshment and relaxation. Relax at opulent spas that provide a variety of therapeutic services, from calming massages to renewing facials. Enjoy the island's relaxing ambience by doing yoga on the beach or meditation in peaceful natural surroundings. Immerse yourself in the spa and wellness activities available on the island, letting the pressures of everyday life to melt away in the midst of the island's natural beauty.

Summer on Amelia Island offers limitless opportunities and unique activities. Whether you're looking for beach pleasure or exhilarating water sports, you've come to the right place.

Amelia Island Foods and Drinks

Amelia Island is a gastronomic paradise that entices the senses with its unique tastes, fresh local ingredients, and inventive culinary creations. From fresh seafood direct from the Atlantic Ocean to international specialties with a local twist, the island's dynamic food and drink scene is a sensory joy. Join us on a delectable journey of Amelia Island's foods and beverages, where every bite and sip is a celebration of culinary excellence.

Extravaganza of Seafood:
Amelia Island, being a seaside resort, offers a plethora of fresh seafood dishes. Savor luscious shrimp, flaky grouper, buttery lobster, and soft crab cakes, all of which highlight the island's marine riches. The island's culinary culture pays respect to the ocean's wonders, from simple seafood shacks providing flawlessly fried baskets of fish and chips to sophisticated restaurants making beautiful seafood dishes.

Lowcountry Cuisine and Southern Comfort:
Discover the soothing aromas of Southern comfort and Lowcountry

cuisine on the menus of Amelia Island's restaurants. Enjoy the smokey scent of slow-cooked barbecue ribs, crunchy fried chicken, and velvety richness of creamy grits. Enjoy traditional delicacies like shrimp and grits, fried green tomatoes, and collard greens, all prepared with Southern friendliness and island charm.

Excellence in Farm-to-Table Cuisine:

Amelia Island embraces the farm-to-table movement, which emphasizes locally produced products. Investigate eateries that emphasize sustainable farming techniques and highlight the island's unique agricultural history. Prepared with fresh, organic veggies, grass-fed meats, and locally caught seafood. Immerse yourself in the bright aromas of fresh foods while also supporting the local farmers that deliver the island's culinary wonders to your table.

International Culinary Journeys:

The cosmopolitan food scene on Amelia Island is a worldwide trip of tastes. Travel to varied gastronomic places in such as Italy, Asia, Mexico, and the Mediterranean. Enjoy handmade pasta, fragrant Thai curries, zingy Mexican street tacos, or delicious Mediterranean kebabs.

Whether you're looking for the spicy spices of Indian food, the delicate tastes of sushi and sashimi, or the tangy citrus notes of ceviche, the island's eclectic culinary options will take you across the globe.

Craft Beers and Mixology Wonders:

Amelia Island is not just a sanctuary for foodies; it also caters to libation connoisseurs. Explore the island's artisan breweries, where professional brewers create one-of-a-kind and tasty beers that capture the character of the island.

While enjoying the laid-back ambience of local brewers, sip on delicious ales, hoppy IPAs, or mellow stouts. Indulge in mixology wonders produced by experienced bartenders that skilfully combine tastes and create inventive drinks utilizing locally obtained ingredients.

Sweet Temptations & Luxurious Desserts:

Without indulging in the island's sweet delights and exquisite desserts, no gastronomic adventure is complete. Enjoy handcrafted ice cream, artisanal chocolates, and freshly baked pastries that display the expertise of the island's pastry chefs.

Enjoy a piece of key lime pie, a Southern pecan pie, or a warm bread pudding drizzled with creamy caramel sauce. These delectable treats will make your taste buds dance and your desires go.

The culinary scene on Amelia Island is a beautiful symphony of tastes, with fresh seafood, Southern comfort, exotic cuisines, and craft libations intertwining to create a stunning gastronomic tapestry.

Amelia Island Archipelago Cruises

Set sail on a unique marine excursion to discover the beautiful Amelia Island Archipelago. This unspoiled collection of islands off the coast of Northeast Florida provides a treasure trove of natural treasures and stunning scenery just waiting to be found.

Join us as we plunge into the turquoise seas and set off on an incredible voyage across the Amelia Island Archipelago, where each island reveals its own distinct beauty and promises a memorable experience.

Expedition to Cumberland Island:

Sail away on an enthralling trip to Cumberland Island, the crown treasure of the Amelia Island Archipelago. This deserted barrier island, rich in history and natural beauty, provides a unique look back in time.

Discover its unspoiled beaches, old marine woods, and the remains of Dungeness, the Carnegie family's stately house. Keep a look out for the island's famed wild horses, which graze freely and give an ethereal touch to the enchantment of the island.

Adventure in the Talbot Islands:

Immerse yourself in the natural magnificence of the Talbot Islands, an archipelago of pristine islands. Cruise along their gorgeous coats, which include quiet beaches, sand dunes, and marine woods.

Anchor in peaceful areas and go on guided nature excursions to see the island's diverse fauna, which includes breeding shorebirds and playful dolphins. Explore the archipelago's hidden coves and secret lagoons by engaging in water sports like kayaking or paddleboarding.

Excursion to Fort George Island:

Discover the historical and cultural riches of Fort George Island, a unique archipelago location. Cruise through the gorgeous canals of the island, appreciating its natural beauty and lovely surroundings.

Visit the Fort George Island Cultural State Park, where the stately historic estate, the Ribault Club, remains as a reminder of the island's rich history. Enjoy the tranquillity of the surroundings and the stunning views of the ocean by taking a leisurely walk around the island's nature paths.

Escape to Little Talbot Island:
Discover the unspoilt splendor of Little Talbot Island, an archipelago's unspoiled sanctuary. Cruise along its gorgeous coastline, where golden sand dunes meet the flowing waves of the Atlantic Ocean.

Anchor near the island's peaceful beaches to relax, swim, and soak up the sun. Explore the island's paths, which snake through unspoiled marine woods, and marvel at the island's plentiful wildlife. Little Talbot Island provides a tranquil haven and a genuine connection with nature.

Intracoastal Waterway Exploration:
Take a lovely trip down the Intracoastal Waterway, which runs through the Amelia Island Archipelago. Sail by breathtaking coastal scenery, private islands, and lovely waterfront villages.

View beautiful beachfront houses, playful dolphins, and majestic ships. This tour offers a fresh viewpoint on the beauty of the archipelago, enabling you to absorb in the calm of the waterway while spending time with loved ones.

Amelia Island Archipelago cruises provide an enthralling journey through a world of natural treasures and tranquil beauty. From the ancient Cumberland Island to the unspoilt Talbot Islands, each place in the archipelago has its own distinct character and guarantees an unforgettable experience.

Explore Cumberland Island's wild horses, immerse yourself in the natural splendor of the Talbot Islands, discover the historical treasures of Fort George Island, escape to the untouched beauty of Little Talbot Island, or cruise along the Intracoastal Waterway.

CHAPTER SIX

AMELIA ISLAND'S NEIGHBORING TOWNS

Fernandina Beach

The major city and entrance to Amelia Island, Fernandina Beach is located on the northern end of the island. It has a historic downtown center, wonderful shops and restaurants, and lovely beaches.

Fernandina Beach, located on the northern end of Amelia Island, is a delightful coastal town that captivates tourists with its historic beauty, stunning surroundings, and active atmosphere.

Fernandina Beach provides a unique combination of natural beauty and cultural riches, from its rich history and architecture to its beautiful beaches and eccentric boutiques. Join us as we explore the enchanting attraction of Fernandina Beach, a coastal jewel that perfectly compliments Amelia Island's magnificence.

Downtown Fernandina Beach's Historic District:

As you walk through the ancient streets of downtown Fernandina Beach, you will be transported back in time. Explore the well-preserved Victorian-era building, which has colorful façade and detailed decorations.

Stroll along Centre Street, which is lined with one-of-a-kind stores, boutiques, and art galleries selling anything from antiques and handcrafted crafts to local artwork and specialized foods. Explore the town's picturesque side streets and absorb its rich history and lively vibe.

Amelia Island History Museum:

The Amelia Island Museum of History will take you on a journey through the fascinating history of Fernandina Beach and Amelia Island. The museum, housed in the historic Nassau County Courthouse, has exhibits that illustrate the island's fascinating history, from Timucua Native Americans through Spanish explorers and the thriving shrimping business.

Discover relics, pictures, and interactive exhibits that highlight the island's history. Don't miss out on the guided tours and unique activities that will give you a better knowledge of the region's cultural heritage.

State Park of Fort Clinch:

Fort Clinch State Park combines the appeal of history and environment. This well-preserved Civil War-era stronghold provides tourists with an insight into the island's military history. Step back in time as you explore the fort's walls, barracks, and stunning seaside vistas.

Take a guided tour to learn about its strategic significance during the Civil War, or watch historical reenactments to be transported back in time. Enjoy the park's beautiful beaches, fishing sites, and nature paths, where you may observe animals and take in the natural beauty of the island.

Beautiful Beaches:

Fernandina Beach is famous for its gorgeous expanses of sandy beachfront, where the Atlantic Ocean invites tourists to rest, swim, and soak up the rays. With its facilities and beachside pavilion,

Main Beach Park is ideal for family picnics and parties.

Secluded areas, such as Peter's Point Beach Park, provide a calm respite for people seeking privacy and spectacular sunsets. Sink your toes into the warm sand, listen to the calming sound of the waves, and let Fernandina Beach's coastal splendor wash over you.

Delights in the Kitchen:

The food scene in Fernandina Beach is a gourmet excursion that tantalizes taste senses with a diversity of tastes. Explore the town's eateries, where chefs highlight the fresh fish from the island in delectable dishes.

Fernandina Beach has something for everyone, from informal seafood shacks serving local favorites like shrimp and oysters to luxury dining venues serving new culinary concoctions. Savor the tastes of the sea and go on a gastronomic adventure that honors the region's seaside charm.

Festivals and Special Events:

Fernandina Beach holds a variety of festivals and events throughout the year to celebrate the town's dynamic culture. A popular event, the Isle of Eight Flags Shrimp Festival, celebrates the island's shrimping legacy with live music, arts and crafts vendors, and, of course, wonderful seafood.

With author readings, book signings, and seminars, the Amelia

Island Book Festival draws literary fans. These festivals and activities bring the community together while also providing an insight into the town's history.

Yulee

Yulee: Yulee is a rising neighborhood west of Amelia Island with a mix of residential and business sectors. It is home to the famous Royal Amelia Golf Course and is conveniently located among other attractions.

Yulee, located just west of Amelia Island, is a calm refuge for those seeking a peaceful getaway from the hectic world. Yulee, surrounded by natural beauty and a friendly ambiance, is the ideal complement to Amelia Island's dynamic vitality. Join us as we explore Yulee's enticing charm, a hidden treasure that begs you to rest, reconnect with nature, and appreciate a slower pace of life.

Wildlife Management Area of Nassau:
Explore the Nassau Wildlife Management Area, a large area of conserved land that highlights the region's unique ecosystems. Nature paths weave through marshes, pine woods, and wetlands, providing

chances for birding, animal observation, and photography. Take in the sights and sounds of this natural refuge as you immerse yourself in the tranquil ambience.

State Forest of Four Creeks:

Discover the raw beauty of the Four Creeks State Forest, a beautiful wilderness near Yulee. This vast forest has picturesque pathways ideal for hiking, bicycling, and equestrian riding. Explore the tranquil quiet of nature by walking along canopied walkways, trickling streams, and towering pines. Discover local creatures, get a sight of brilliant flowers, and relax in the tranquility that the forest provides.

State Park on Big Talbot Island:

Travel east to Big Talbot Island State Park, a coastal sanctuary with stunning landscapes and unusual geological formations. Explore the park's coastal woods, sandy beaches, and salt marshes, which are home to a variety of habitats. Explore the famed "Boneyard Beach," which is covered with old, aged trees and bleached driftwood, creating a magical scene right out of a storybook. Capture the ethereal splendor of the seashore and revel in the seclusion of this enthralling seaside haven.

The Kingsley Plantation:

Visit the Kingsley Plantation, a National Historic Landmark in

Yulee, to learn about the region's history. This beautifully-preserved mansion offers insight into the lives of enslaved people as well as the plantation's complicated past. Explore the plantation home, slave quarters, and surrounding grounds, where historical tales are brought to life. Guided tours and exhibitions provide further information about the plantation's history and the individuals who helped develop it.

Outdoor Activities:

Yulee's closeness to nature gives plenty of chances for outdoor lovers. Launch your boat or kayak into the Nassau River or Lofton Creek, where you may discover secret coves and negotiate the tranquil waters. Fish in the many freshwater lakes or throw a line along the riverbanks in search of a coveted catch. Yulee's natural settings entice you to walk, ride, or picnic in its parks, instilling both calm and adventure.

Charm & Hospitality in the Neighborhood:

Yulee's small-town charm is reflected in its local businesses and genuine friendliness. Explore small stores and boutiques for one-of-a-kind treasures, handcrafted crafts, and locally produced items.

Enjoy regional delicacies at family-owned restaurants and diners, where friendly faces and great meals await. Participate in local events and festivals when the community gets together to celebrate its history and develop a feeling of community.

Yulee, a tranquil refuge just beyond Amelia Island's shoreline, provides a haven of natural beauty, rich history, and kind hospitality. Whether you want to find peace in the undisturbed nature, learn about the region's history, or just relax in a small-town ambiance, this is the place to be.

Nassauville

Nassauville is a tiny village southwest of Amelia Island noted for its peaceful residential subdivisions and closeness to the Nassau River. It provides a tranquil setting with convenient access to outdoor leisure activities.

Nassauville, located southwest of Amelia Island, enables tourists to explore a hidden treasure of solitude and natural beauty. Nassauville, surrounded by beautiful surroundings and the lovely Nassau River, provides a tranquil respite from the hectic world, enabling guests to immerse themselves in the mesmerizing ambience of this quaint coastal town. Join us as we explore

Nassauville's allure, where leisure, outdoor experiences, and a feeling of peace await.

The Nassau River:

Nassauville's closeness to the beautiful Nassau River is one of its charms. Explore the peaceful waters of this natural river by taking a leisurely boat trip or renting a kayak. Drift down the flowing rivers, surrounded by lush marshes and towering trees, and soak in the tranquillity. Keep a look out for the river's natural fauna, which includes dolphins, manatees, and a variety of bird species. The Nassau River is a nature lover's paradise, providing a serene setting for wonderful encounters.

Trails for Biking and Hiking:

Nassauville is bordered by beautiful pathways that invite outdoor lovers to discover the region's natural beauties. Lace up your hiking boots or get on your bike and explore the nearby conservation areas. As you go through woods, marshes, and coastal hammocks, you'll come upon hidden treasures. Nassauville's paths provide the ideal blend of excitement and tranquillity, enabling you to connect with nature while taking in the spectacular scenery.

Hammock in Nassauville:

Wander through the Nassauville Hammock, a conserved woodland area that displays the region's unique flora and animals, to enter a magical world. Wander the shady paths, enjoying the fragrances of pine trees and listening to the soothing rustling of leaves above. The hammock is home to a wide variety of fauna, including deer, gopher tortoises, and many bird species. Take a minute to admire the natural beauty of this paradise and connect with the serene spirit that surrounds you.

Water Sports and Recreation:
Those who appreciate fishing and water sports will find plenty of possibilities to throw a line or set sail in Nassauville. Explore the Nassau Sound and neighboring inlets for a plethora of fish species. Join a fishing boat or try your luck from the beach, soaking in the anticipation of a possible catch. If you want to take it easy, rent a paddleboard or kayak and explore the calm waters at your own speed, taking in the beauty of the surrounding coastal area.

Charm & Hospitality in the Neighborhood:
Nassauville's small-town charm and friendly welcome make tourists feel at home. Explore local stores and boutiques for one-of-a-kind treasures, artwork, and souvenirs. Connect with friendly locals who are keen to share their enthusiasm for the region and provide tips on hidden treasures and lesser-known attractions.

Don't pass up the chance to dine at one of Nassauville's lovely restaurants, where fresh seafood and local tastes take center stage, assuring a delectable culinary experience.

Amelia Island's entry point:
Nassauville serves as the island's entrance, allowing easy access to the island's attractions and facilities. Visitors may explore the island's magnificent beaches, revel in its culinary pleasures, and learn about its rich history and lively culture all within a short drive. The strategic position of Nassauville enables you to enjoy the best of both worlds: a calm getaway in the middle of nature and convenient access to the exciting amenities of Amelia Island.

O'Neil

Located northwest of Amelia Island, O'Neil is a rural community with a laid-back attitude. It has a diverse natural environment that includes marshes, waterways, and wooded regions. O'Neil is popular among nature lovers and those looking for a peaceful escape.

O'Neil, a hidden treasure northwest of Amelia Island, provides a tranquil vacation surrounded by pristine scenery and a calm environment. O'Neil urges tourists to rest, reconnect with nature, and appreciate a slower pace of life with its quiet appeal and wealth of natural beauty. Join us as we explore O'Neil's enchantment, where pure nature, stunning landscapes, and a feeling of peace await.

Paradise Found in Nature:

With its huge range of unspoilt landscapes and pure wildness, O'Neil is a nature lover's delight. Explore the magnificent nature paths that weave through deep woods, peaceful rivers, and lovely marshes in the region. Immerse yourself in the natural splendor of O'Neil as you experience local species ranging from magnificent birds flying above to lively otters and deer roaming freely. O'Neil's untouched environment welcomes you to immerse yourself in its peacefulness, whether hiking, riding, or just wandering along the paths.

Sheffield Wildlife Management Area consists of the following areas:

The Sheffield animals Management Area, which is next to O'Neil, provides a haven for animals as well as outdoor lovers. The area's various ecosystems, which include wetlands, pine woods, and open fields, make it ideal for birding, animal viewing, and photography.

Photograph uncommon bird species in flight or witness secretive creatures in their native habitats. Sheffield Wildlife Management Area is a hidden treasure waiting to be found by anyone seeking a closer relationship with nature.

Amelia Island State Park:

Amelia Island State Park, a short distance away, entices tourists with its unspoilt shoreline and lovely beaches. Explore the park's pristine coastline, where you may walk along kilometers of sandy beaches, gather seashells, and bask in the sun's warm embrace. Enjoy a range of leisure activities by the water's edge, such as picnics, fishing, or horseback riding. Amelia Island State Park is a peaceful haven away from the people, where you may relax and take in the natural beauty that surrounds you.

Swamp of Okefenokee:

O'Neil is close to the famed Okefenokee Swamp, which provides a genuinely authentic wilderness experience. Set off on an amazing journey across this enormous wilderness, which is known for its natural marshes, cypress trees, and plentiful animals. Canoe or kayak across the swamp's network of rivers, taking in the beautiful splendor of this pristine nature. Listen to the symphony of birdsong, catch views of alligators lazing in the sun, and wonder at the gorgeous reflections produced by the cypress trees that surround you. The Okefenokee Swamp is a nature lover's paradise.

Fishing and other outdoor activities:

O'Neil's closeness to the Nassau River and other nearby waterways affords several options for fishing and other outdoor activities. Cast a line from the riverbank, join a fishing charter, or launch your boat into the tranquil waters for an exciting day of fishing. The abundance of fish species in the region ensures a gratifying experience for both experienced and novice fishermen. Outdoor enthusiasts may also participate in sports like as kayaking, paddleboarding, and boating, which enable them to immerse themselves in the peacefulness of O'Neil's natural surroundings.

Local Hospitality and Appeal:

O'Neil emanates authentic small-town charm and kind friendliness, making tourists feel right at home. Explore local stores and markets for one-of-a-kind crafts, fresh vegetables, and locally created items. Engage with friendly locals who are keen to share their enthusiasm for the region and give ideas for hidden jewels and off-the-beaten-path attractions.

Others are:

American Beach is located south of Amelia Island and is historically significant as one of the few beachside neighborhoods available to African Americans during the period of segregation. It has a rich cultural past, gorgeous beaches, and is a popular sunbathing and picnics destination.

Kingsland, Georgia: Kingsland is a Georgia city located just over the state border, north of Amelia Island. It gives easy access to the island and acts as a gateway for visitors coming from the north. Kingsland has a range of services, such as stores, restaurants, and lodging.

St. Marys, Georgia: St. Marys is a scenic coastal hamlet northeast of Amelia Island recognized for its attractive downtown area and close to the Cumberland Island National Seashore. It has historical attractions, seaside parks, and beautiful river vistas.

Jacksonville, Florida: Located south of Amelia Island, Jacksonville is Florida's biggest city and offers a variety of facilities, cultural attractions, and entertainment alternatives. It has a dynamic downtown center, active neighborhoods, and magnificent beaches.

These Amelia Island neighboring locations provide extra options for exploration, leisure, and cultural experiences, increasing the overall guest experience and expanding the diversity of activities accessible in the region.

CHAPTER SEVEN

OTHER NOTABLE ACTIVITIES TOURIST MUST CHECK OUT

7-Day Itinerary For Tourist To Amelia Island

Welcome to Amelia Island, a charming coastal destination brimming with history, natural beauty, and genuine friendliness.
This 7-day tour will take you on a remarkable voyage across the island's rich past, magnificent scenery, gastronomic pleasures, and pristine beaches. Prepare to make wonderful memories as you start on a week-long trip in Amelia Island's fascinating environment.

Day 1: Arrival at Historic Fernandina Beach:
Arrive to Amelia Island and check into your hotel.
Begin your adventure by visiting Fernandina Beach's historic downtown neighborhood.

Explore Centre Street, which is lined with one-of-a-kind stores, boutiques, and art galleries.

Visit the Amelia Island Museum of History to learn about the island's fascinating history.

Savor the tastes of the island's fresh seafood with a great supper at a local restaurant.

Day 2: Visit The Fort Clinch State Park and Beaches on:

Begin your day by visiting Fort Clinch State Park, where you can tour the well-preserved Civil War-era fortification and take in the gorgeous coastline vistas.

Spend the day soaking up the sun and swimming in the crystal-clear seas on the island's immaculate beaches.

Participate in water sports such as kayaking, paddleboarding, or an exciting jet ski trip.

In the evening, watch a beautiful sunset on the beach for a picture-perfect ending to the day.

Day 3: Explore Nature and Wildlife in Amelia Island

Take an eco-tour to learn about Amelia Island's unique habitats and fauna.

Explore the island's nature paths, such as Egan's Creek Greenway and Amelia Island State Park, to observe natural plants and species.

Take a lovely boat excursion across the canals, looking for dolphins, manatees, and other bird species.

Immerse yourself in nature's serene splendor by having a picnic in one of the island's picturesque parks.

Day 4: Check Out The Cumberland Island National Seashore:

Take a day excursion to Cumberland Island, which is accessible by ferry from Amelia Island.

Discover the remains of Dungeness, the Carnegie family's stately estate, as well as the island's stunning beaches and marine woodlands.

As you explore the natural splendor of this remote haven, keep an eye out for the island's famed wild horses.

Before returning to Amelia Island, stop for a picnic lunch in the middle of Cumberland Island's natural beauty.

Day 5: Have Some Culinary Delights and Cultural Experiences:

Visit local eateries ranging from simple seafood shacks to luxury dining venues to immerse yourself in Amelia Island's culinary culture.

Take a gastronomic walking tour to experience the flavors of the island and learn about its food culture.

Discover fresh fruit, artisanal items, and local crafts at the farmers market.

Immerse yourself in the island's lively arts scene by attending a cultural event or live performance.

Day 6: Enjoy Some Outdoor Activities

Start your day off right by renting bikes or taking a guided bike tour to discover Amelia Island's gorgeous trails and coastal routes.

Water activities like as paddleboarding, kayaking, and surfing may be enjoyed along the island's gorgeous shoreline.

Enjoy spectacular vistas while navigating tough fairways at one of the island's top golf courses.

Relax in the afternoon with a spa treatment or wellness activity that will revitalize your mind, body, and spirit.

Day 7: Enjoy Beach Bliss Before Leaving

Spend your last day relaxing on Amelia Island's beautiful beaches.

Soak up the rays, swim in the clear waters, and enjoy beachfront picnics or seaside restaurants.

Take a leisurely beach stroll, gathering seashells and enjoying the peaceful atmosphere.

Bid Amelia Island goodbye, cherishing the memories made over your memorable 7-day visit.

Amelia Island is a lovely getaway rich in history, natural beauty, and coastal charm. This 7-day trip offers a thorough experience, enabling you to immerse yourself in the island's intriguing attractions, appreciate its culinary pleasures, and relax on its beautiful beaches.

Amelia Island delivers a week of magic and lifetime memories, whether you're seeing historic places, going into nature, engaging in gourmet excursions, or just resting on the beach.

Tips and Information You Must Know Before Visiting Amelia Island

Exploring Amelia Island is an exciting possibility, with infinite opportunities for exploration, relaxation, and pleasure.

To guarantee a pleasant and memorable experience, arm yourself with useful knowledge and helpful hints. We'll present you with crucial facts, insider insights, and practical guidance in this complete guide to help you make the most of your stay on Amelia Island.

How to Get to Amelia Island:
Amelia Island's location in Northeast Florida makes it readily accessible by numerous modes of transportation. If you're flying in, the nearest major airport is Jacksonville International Airport

(JAX), which is about 30 miles southwest of Amelia Island.

The most convenient alternative is to rent a vehicle or take a cab from the airport. Amelia Island is also easily accessible by automobile through major roads, making it a popular destination for road excursions.

Temperature and Best Times to Visit:

Amelia Island has a lovely subtropical climate with mild winters and warm summers. The optimum time to visit is determined by your own tastes. Spring and autumn provide comfortable temperatures, less people, and vivid natural scenery.

Summers might be hot and humid, but they provide plenty of beach activities and water sports. Winter is a calmer season, perfect for people looking for a relaxing getaway. Remember that hurricane season lasts from June to November, so keep updated about weather conditions throughout this period.

Language and currency:

The United States Dollar (USD) is the currency used in Amelia Island and across the United States. Although credit cards are routinely accepted, it is always a good idea to have some cash on hand for minor purchases or in case of an emergency. Because English is the predominant language spoken on

Amelia Island, communicating with English-speaking guests is simple.

On-Island Transportation:

Getting to Amelia Island is simple and easy. Renting a vehicle is a popular alternative since it enables you to explore the island at your own speed. Taxis, ride-sharing services, and shuttle services are also available for airport transportation or shorter distances. Many sights, restaurants, and stores, particularly in the historic downtown center, are within walking or bicycling distance.

Accommodations:

Amelia Island has a variety of lodging options to meet any traveler's interests and budget. There are alternatives for every taste, from luxury beachside resorts and boutique hotels to vacation rentals and homey bed and breakfasts. Booking your lodgings well in advance is recommended, particularly during high seasons or if you have specific preferences.

Security and safety:

Amelia Island is recognized for its pleasant and safe atmosphere, but you should always take steps to protect your safety. Keep your valuables protected and be aware of your surroundings, particularly in busy places.

It's a good idea to get acquainted with emergency contact numbers as well as the location of the closest hospital or medical institution. Follow safety standards and be aware of any possible dangers if you want to participate in water activities or visit natural regions.

Local Regulations and Laws:
When visiting Amelia Island, it is essential to get acquainted with the local rules and regulations. Follow traffic laws, such as speed limits, seatbelt use, and parking requirements.

Respect local customs and traditions, and keep noise levels in mind, especially in residential areas. In addition, follow beach rules, such as those prohibiting open fires, alcohol drinking, and the conservation of animals and natural environments.

Beach Etiquette and Outdoor Activities:
Natural beauty and outdoor activities are among Amelia Island's most treasured features. Follow beach etiquette principles such as tidying up after yourself, not littering, and respecting the environment and animals while visiting the beaches. Before swimming or engaging in water sports, check with local authorities or lifeguards about any safety issues or beach conditions.

Investigating the Historic District:
The historic downtown district of Fernandina Beach is a must-see

when visiting Amelia Island. Wear comfortable shoes for touring the historic neighborhood since you will be walking a lot.

Explore the lovely streets, enjoy the well-preserved architecture, and discover the unique stores and boutiques. Don't forget to taste the local food and revel in the gastronomic delicacies of the island.

Outdoor Recreation:

Outdoor aficionados will love Amelia Island. It is important to be prepared while trekking through natural paths, riding along picturesque roads, or participating in water activities. Wear attire and footwear suited for the activities you want to participate in.

Wear sunscreen, a hat, and sunglasses to protect yourself from the sun. Keep hydrated and have water with you, particularly in hot weather. Respect the natural environment by leaving no trace and protecting it for future generations.

Dining and cooking:

Amelia Island has a thriving culinary culture, with eating choices to suit every taste and budget. The island's restaurants provide a wide variety of cuisines, from fresh seafood to foreign cuisine.

Make reservations in advance for popular restaurants or at busy periods while dining out. Consider visiting local farmers markets to get fresh food and handcrafted items.

Service Charges and Tipping:
Tipping is expected across the United States, including Amelia Island. Tipping waitstaff, bartenders, hotel staff, and taxi drivers is typical.

Safety Tips for Tourists To Amelia Island

Amelia Island, with its attractive coastal environment and stunning scenery, is a tranquil and welcome destination for visitors. While the island is well-known for its safety and friendliness, it is important to prioritize your safety and take the required steps to guarantee a pleasant and worry-free vacation.
Here're some vital safety information and practical recommendations in this guide to help you make the most of your stay on Amelia Island.

Keep Up to Date:
Research the most recent travel warnings and safety information about Amelia Island before your trip. For updates on any possible problems, weather conditions, or special safety suggestions, check

your government's travel website or contact trusted sources. Staying educated will allow you to make more informed choices and guarantee a more pleasant experience.

Protect Your Property:
It is critical to safeguard your personal things in order to have a safe journey. Keep valuables, such as passports, cash, and devices, in a safe place, such as a hotel safe or a hidden travel bag. When touring the island, avoid bringing huge quantities of cash and unneeded items. To combat pickpockets or opportunistic theft, be aware of your surroundings and carry locked bags or backpacks.

Transportation Security:
If you use public transportation, such as taxis or ride-sharing services, be sure it is legal and reliable. If you're renting a car, make sure it's locked and that no valuables are visible inside. Follow driving laws, including speed restrictions, and wear seat belts at all times. To guarantee a safe and pleasant driving experience, be vigilant and respect all traffic signs and laws.

Water Safety:
The beaches and water activities on Amelia Island are popular with tourists. Practice water safety precautions when enjoying the ocean. Swim only in specified locations and keep an eye out for

any caution signs suggesting dangerous circumstances. Consider using a life jacket if you are not a good swimmer.

Pay heed to lifeguards' advice and follow any posted safety restrictions. Follow local restrictions and utilize suitable safety equipment while participating in water sports or boating activities.

Protection against the sun:

The bright environment of Amelia Island necessitates adequate sun protection. To protect yourself from damaging UV rays, use sunscreen with a high SPF rating and wear a hat, sunglasses, and lightweight protective clothes.

Seek cover during peak sun exposure hours, which are generally between 10 a.m. and 4 p.m. Staying hydrated by drinking enough water is particularly important in hot weather.

Wildlife and natural areas must be respected:

Amelia Island is home to a variety of natural ecosystems and fauna. Respect the island's environment by keeping a safe distance from wildlife and refraining from feeding or disturbing it. Follow any animal conservation notices and instructions that are displayed.

Avoid littering and leaving no trace to protect the environment. Preserve the natural beauty of the island for future generations to enjoy.

Emergency Planning:
Learn the emergency phone numbers for your local police, fire agency, and medical services. Make a mental note of the closest hospital or medical facility, and have a first-aid kit on hand in case of minor accidents or illnesses. Consider obtaining travel insurance that includes coverage for medical emergencies, trip cancellations, and lost or stolen items.

Personal Security:
While Amelia Island is typically secure, it is vital to use caution and be aware of your surroundings. At night, stay in well-lit locations and avoid wandering alone in remote or unknown regions. Travel with a partner or join scheduled trips if you want to explore the island after dark.

Trust your intuition and avoid circumstances that make you feel uneasy. Share your itinerary and contact details with a trustworthy family member or friend back home.

Water and Beach Activities:
Be careful while engaging in beach and water sports, particularly if you are not a great swimmer if the ocean is turbulent. Pay attention to any safety instructions given by lifeguards or activity operators.

When hiring a boat or engaging in water activities, be sure the equipment is in excellent shape and that you get sufficient instructions on how to use it and safety precautions.

Hygiene and health:

Good hygiene measures are critical for a safe and healthy travel. Wash your hands often, particularly before eating and after visiting public restrooms. Carry hand sanitizer with you in case soap and water are unavailable.

Drink bottled water or use a water filter system to stay hydrated. Carry any essential medicines and see your healthcare professional before flying if you have any pre-existing medical issues.

Amelia Island provides a calm and pleasant atmosphere for visitors, with safety and security as top priorities. You may have a safe and worry-free vacation by remaining informed, securing your possessions, following aquatic safety procedures, and using common sense.

Remember to emphasize your well-being, respect the natural environment of the island, and create lasting memories on this stunning seaside getaway.

Uber Security in Amelia Island

Uber has become a popular mode of transportation for tourists, offering quick and dependable trips in many locations across the globe, including Amelia Island.

When using Uber in Amelia Island, prioritize your safety and take the essential procedures to guarantee a safe and enjoyable ride. In this article, we'll look at the safety procedures and tools offered by Uber to improve your security when traveling on Amelia Island.

Unverified Drivers:

Uber's stringent driver verification procedure is one of its most important security elements. Uber does thorough background checks on all prospective drivers, including criminal records and driving histories. This helps to guarantee that only qualified and trustworthy people become Amelia Island Uber drivers.

Driver's Evaluations and Comments:

Following each Uber journey, clients may evaluate their driver and leave comments on their experience. This strategy encourages responsibility and aids in the maintenance of a high level of service quality. Drivers who have repeatedly poor ratings or complaints may be reviewed and perhaps removed from the Uber platform.

Trip Sharing and GPS Tracking:

Uber has a GPS tracking technology that enables you to follow your journey in real time through the Uber app. This tool assures transparency and adds an extra degree of protection by enabling you to share travel information with friends and family. You may quickly share your trip status with your trusted contacts, including the driver's name, car details, and projected arrival time.

Accountability on both sides:

Uber has a two-way accountability mechanism in place. Passengers may rate drivers, but drivers can also rate passengers. This helps both parties maintain a courteous and safe atmosphere. To ensure a great and secure experience, it is critical that you treat your driver with respect and follow Uber's community rules.

Safety features in-app:

Uber is always investing in safety measures inside its app to improve passenger security. These features may differ based on your region and the Uber app version you're using. In-app safety features include the ability to share your trip status with emergency contacts, an emergency help button that connects you with local authorities, and the opportunity to report safety problems directly to Uber.

Customer Service and Support:

Uber's app and website provide specialized customer care and help. If you have any questions or encounter any problems during your journey, you may call Uber's support staff for help. They are accessible 24 hours a day, 7 days a week and can answer any inquiries or resolve any safety concerns you may have.

Personal Safety Recommendations:

While Uber aims to provide a safe and secure platform, riders must also take personal safety measures. Check that the license plate, driver's name, and car model match the information supplied on the app before entering the vehicle. Always choose the rear seat for more personal space and a clear line of sight. Trust your intuition and, if required, disclose any concerns to friends, family, or authorities.

Uber is a dependable and convenient mode of transportation for visitors to Amelia Island. Uber stresses passenger security via its driver certification process, GPS monitoring, two-way accountability, and in-app safety measures. You may have a safe and pleasurable journey on Amelia Island by following personal safety rules and using Uber's safety features.

Tips For Visiting Amelia Island on a Tight Budget

Visiting Amelia Island does not have to be expensive. You may enjoy the island's natural beauty, rich history, and lively culture while remaining within your budget with a little forethought and wise decision-making.

Here're some helpful information and insider ideas that will help you make the most of your Amelia Island journey without sacrificing amazing experiences. Prepare to go on an inexpensive adventure loaded with engaging sights, delectable food, and treasured memories.

Accommodation:

Consider staying in a budget-friendly lodging such as a vacation rental, a guesthouse, or a cheap hotel. Booking ahead of time and being flexible with your trip dates may often result in big discounts.

Furthermore, looking for choices just outside of the major tourist districts might provide more cheap prices without losing comfort or convenience.

Dining:

Experiencing the island's gastronomic marvels does not have to be expensive. Look for local restaurants, food trucks, or informal seafood shacks that provide tasty meals at affordable costs.

Take advantage of happy hour specials or lunch menus, which sometimes provide lower-priced versions of popular meals. Exploring the local farmers market is another excellent opportunity to enjoy fresh food and handmade items while also supporting local sellers.

Activities that are free or low-cost:

Amelia Island has a multitude of free or low-cost activities that enable you to immerse yourself in the island's beauty without breaking the bank. Explore the island's beaches and take leisurely walks along the coastline, collecting seashells and admiring the spectacular sunsets.

Explore Fernandina Beach's historic area, strolling through its charming streets and admiring the well-preserved buildings. Visit the Amelia Island Museum of History on free entry days, or explore the island's many parks and nature trails for a low-cost outdoor experience.

Outdoor Activities:

Take advantage of Amelia Island's natural beauty by participating in low-cost outdoor activities. Pack a picnic and spend the day exploring the historic fort, hiking gorgeous trails, and relaxing on the beach at Fort Clinch State Park.

Rent bicycles and explore the island's beautiful neighborhoods and scenic surroundings at your leisure. Alternatively, spend a relaxing day fishing or birding, connecting with nature and taking in the tranquility of the island.

Festivals and cultural events:

Throughout the year, Amelia Island holds a number of cultural events and festivals, many of which are free or low-cost to attend. Check the local events calendar to see if your visit coincides with any of these exciting festivals.

There's plenty for everyone to enjoy without breaking the bank, from music festivals and art exhibits to culinary markets and historical reenactments.

Investigate Amelia Island's History:

Take self-directed walking excursions or participate in economical guided tours to learn about Amelia Island's rich history. Explore the island's history by visiting historic landmarks such as the Old Town Cemetery, the

Amelia Island Lighthouse, and the many monuments and plaques that give information about the island's fascinating history.

Many of these historical locations may be visited for free or for a little price, making it an enriching and economical experience.

Transportation:

To go about the island, use low-cost transportation choices. Walking or bicycling around the picturesque streets of Fernandina Beach and its neighboring regions is a terrific way to explore.

Many sights and facilities are within walking distance, enabling you to save money on transportation. Public transportation, like buses or shuttles, may also provide cost-effective ways to move about the island.

Take Advantage of Special Offers & Discounts:

Keep an eye out for special offers, discounts, and deals from local companies, attractions, and tour operators.

Check their websites, social media accounts, or contact them directly to learn about any current promotions or discounted rates. Group discounts, coupons, and packaged packages might help you stretch your budget even further and enjoy many events for less money.

Pack Wisely and Save:

Packing wisely will help you save money on your trip to Amelia Island. Bring necessities like sunscreen, bug repellent, and reusable water bottles to avoid paying inflated tourist rates.

Pack snacks or picnic items to enjoy meals on the road and save money on eating out. Bring suitable walking shoes, a hat, and a reusable shopping bag in case you make any local purchases.

Visiting Amelia Island on a budget allows you to explore the island's beauty and attraction without sacrificing remarkable experiences. You may discover the island's natural beauty, delight in local food, and immerse yourself in its rich history and colorful culture while keeping your pocketbook happy if you follow these budget-friendly ideas. Embrace Amelia Island's beauty without breaking the wallet, and make treasured experiences that will last a lifetime.

Top 12 things Tourist Should Do in Amelia Island

Explore Fernandina Beach's Historic Downtown:

Discover the picturesque streets of Fernandina Beach's historic center, which are packed with quaint boutiques, art galleries, and Victorian-era buildings. Stroll along Centre Street, visit interesting stores, and learn about the fascinating history of this region.

Explore Fort Clinch State Park:

Fort Clinch State Park, a well-preserved Civil War-era stronghold, transports you back in time. Explore the fort's exhibits, enjoy a guided tour, and see historical reenactments. Within the park, you may enjoy nature walks, bike pathways, and stunning beaches.

Relax on the Beautiful Beaches:

Amelia Island has miles of gorgeous, sandy beaches on which to relax and soak up the sun. Whether you're looking for quiet or enjoyment, the island's beaches are ideal for swimming, sunbathing, beachcombing, and water sports.

Take a Beach Horseback Riding Adventure:

A horseback ride down the beach allows you to appreciate the beauty of Amelia Island's shoreline. The calm of the beach may be enjoyed while making amazing memories atop a gorgeous horse on guided trips.

Visit Amelia Island State Park:

Amelia Island State Park is a nature lover's paradise. Hike

gorgeous trails, ride along seaside roads, and see wildlife in its natural environment. This clean and protected region is ideal for picnics, fishing, and birding.

The Amelia Island Museum of History is a must-see:

The Amelia Island Museum of History will take you on a journey through the island's unique history. Learn about the region's unique legacy via interactive displays that highlight Native American artifacts, Spanish colonization, the Gilded Age, and other topics.

Go on a Sunset Cruise:

On a romantic sunset cruise, you may see the amazing splendor of an Amelia Island sunset. Enjoy breathtaking vistas, soft breezes, and the bright hues of the evening sun on a boat excursion.

Learn about Cumberland Island National Seashore:

Take a day excursion to Cumberland Island, which can be reached by ferry from Amelia Island. Discover this unspoiled environment, which is home to wild horses, beautiful beaches, and old ruins. Hike through marine woods and see the natural treasures of the island.

Take part in water sports:

Amelia Island has a variety of water activities for thrill seekers. Attempt kayaking, paddleboarding, surfing, or jet skiing. Whether you're a novice or a seasoned water enthusiast, the island's coastline waters provide limitless opportunities for fun and excitement.

Consume Local Cuisine:

Explore the culinary scene of Amelia Island. Local seafood eateries provide fresh seafood ranging from exquisite prawns to scrumptious oysters. Don't pass up the chance to sample Southern favorites like fried green tomatoes and Lowcountry boil, which are served with a delightful drink of sweet tea.

Play a Golf Game:

Amelia Island is a golfer's dream, with world-class courses set in magnificent natural settings. Enjoy panoramic vistas as you tee off on immaculate courses in this golfer's paradise.

Learn about local art and culture:

Immerse yourself in the rich artistic culture of the island. Visit art galleries exhibiting local and regional talent, see live performances at the Amelia Island Theater, or learn about seminars and programs at the Amelia Island Arts Academy.

Amelia Island has a wide range of activities for tourists looking for a mix of history, natural beauty, outdoor adventures, and cultural pleasures.

This wonderful island offers something for everyone, from

visiting the ancient downtown center to resting on magnificent beaches, immersing yourself in local history and cuisine, and enjoying exhilarating water sports. Embrace Amelia Island's charm and make lifetime memories by participating in these top 12 activities.

Top 10 Delicious Foods to Try in Amelia Island

Fresh Seafood:
Amelia Island is well-known for its delicious seafood. Succulent shrimp, delectable oysters, and tasty fish dishes taken directly from the Atlantic Ocean. Don't pass up a classic shrimp boil or a delectable seafood platter at one of the island's numerous seafood eateries.

Lowcountry Stew:
With a hearty Lowcountry boil, you can immerse yourself in the flavors of the Lowcountry. This traditional Southern meal combines shrimp, sausage, corn on the cob, and potatoes simmered in a fragrant mix of spices. It's a real comfort food experience that embodies the area.

Burgers de luxe:
Sink your teeth into a flavor-packed gourmet burger. Amelia

Island's restaurants offer a wide range of inventive burgers, from juicy Angus beef patties to unusual combinations like brie and caramelized onions, bacon jam and blue cheese, or avocado and sriracha aioli. For the ultimate comfort food experience, pair your burger with a side of hand-cut fries.

Fried Green Tomatoes in the South:

Try fried green tomatoes, a traditional Southern treat. These acidic, unripe tomatoes are fried to perfection in a crunchy cornmeal batter. They provide a delicious combination of textures and tastes whether served as an appetizer or side dish.

Soup with She-Crab:

Enjoy the rich and creamy tastes of She-Crab Soup, a traditional meal from the South's coastal areas. This silky bisque is made with blue crab meat, crab roe, cream, and a dash of sherry, resulting in a delicious and soothing soup that will satisfy seafood fans.

Biscuits and Gravy of the Southern Style:

Begin the day with a typical Southern breakfast of fluffy biscuits slathered in creamy sausage gravy. This rich and savory meal is a Southern favorite that will keep you nourished for a day of visiting Amelia Island.

Pie with Key Lime:

A piece of zesty and delicious Key Lime Pie will satisfy your sweet taste. This traditional Florida dessert, made with fresh Key lime juice and a buttery graham cracker crust, is the ideal finish to a fantastic dinner. For an added pleasure, top it with a dab of whipped cream.

Shrimp with Grits:

A meal of shrimp and grits is the ultimate comfort food. On a bed of creamy, stone-ground grits seasoned with bacon, herbs, and spices, succulent shrimp are presented. For anyone looking for a taste of Southern cuisine, this rich and savory meal is a must-try.

Freshly Baked Pastries:

Begin your day by visiting a local bakery and indulging in freshly made pastries. From flaky croissants and buttery danishes to luscious cinnamon buns and fruit-filled turnovers, Amelia Island bakeries provide a delectable selection of sweets to satiate your needs.

Artisanal beer:

A pint of artisan beer from one of the island's brewers will quench your thirst. Amelia Island's craft beer culture is thriving, with beers to suit every taste. You'll discover the right beverage to suit your culinary experiences, from hoppy IPAs to silky stouts and pleasant ales.

Amelia Island is a foodie's heaven, with a wide variety of cuisines and gourmet experiences. The island's culinary culture will tempt your taste buds with everything from fresh seafood delights to cozy Southern favorites and enticing desserts.

Immerse yourself in Amelia Island's delicacies and go on a gastronomic adventure that will leave you wanting more.

Travel Packs You Must Have While Visiting Amelia Island

Having the correct travel pack for your trip to Amelia Island is vital for ease, organization, and comfort. A well-equipped travel pack can make your vacation even more delightful, whether you're visiting the island's beaches, going on outdoor excursions, or meandering through historic downtown Fernandina Beach.

This tutorial will go through the important components of a functional and efficient travel pack, as well as examples and the best materials to use.

Daypack or Backpack:

The core of a dependable travel pack is a robust and comfortable backpack or daypack. Look for a backpack that has adjustable shoulder straps, a cushioned back panel, and various sections for simple organizing.

Choose a size that is appropriate for your requirements, whether it is a little daypack or a bigger backpack for extended trips.

The Osprey Talon 22 Backpack, for example, is a lightweight and adaptable alternative with a hydration reservoir and a comfortable fit.

Wallet or Organizer for Travel:

Using a travel wallet or organizer, you can keep your vital trip papers, such as passports, IDs, tickets, and itineraries, secure and conveniently accessible. To secure your personal information from unwanted scanning, look for one that has RFID-blocking technology.

The Bellroy Travel Wallet, for example, has designated sections for passports, cards, cash, and boarding tickets, allowing you to easily access all of your important papers.

Cubes for packing:

Packing cubes help you save room while staying organized. These lightweight zippered compartments assist you in separating and categorizing your clothing and things, making it simpler to locate what you need without having to unload your whole bag.

The Eagle Creek Pack-It Specter Cube Set, for example, features various-sized cubes constructed of robust and water-resistant plastic to keep your things neatly packed and protected.

Reusable Water Bottle:

Staying hydrated is essential, particularly in the Florida heat. Carry a reusable water bottle with you to prevent waste and ensure you have access to water during your Amelia Island travels. Look for a bottle that is long-lasting, leak-proof, and simple to clean.

The Hydro Flask Wide Mouth Bottle, for example, has double-wall vacuum insulation to keep beverages cool for hours and a stainless steel structure to provide durability for outdoor activities.

Toiletry Bag:

Pack your basic essentials in a small, spill-resistant toiletry bag. Look for one that has many compartments, transparent bags for easy sight, and waterproof materials to keep any leaks contained.

The Sea to Summit Travelling Light Hanging Toiletry Bag, for example, has plenty of storage space and a handy hanging hook, enabling you to conveniently reach your amenities while keeping them tidy and safe.

Charger on the Go:

Using a portable charger, you can ensure that you never miss a picture opportunity or lose connectivity while on your trips. Look for one with many USB ports and a large enough battery.

For example, the Anker PowerCore Portable Charger has quick charging capabilities and can charge several devices at the same time, allowing you to stay connected on the go.

First-Aid Kit for Travel:

With a little first aid pack, you may be ready for minor crises. Include bandages, antiseptic wipes, pain relievers, and other drugs required for your unique requirements.

The Adventure Medical Kits Ultralight & Watertight First Aid Kit, for example, is a lightweight and small choice that includes a variety of medical supplies for common accidents and illnesses.

A well-organized and intelligently prepared travel bag may make or break your trip to Amelia Island. The correct gear improves your experience, from a dependable bag to keep your possessions safe to packing cubes that make locating goods a snap. When choosing your travel pack components, keep comfort, organization, and durability in mind. With the correct equipment, you'll be able to visit Amelia Island's magnificent beaches, historical monuments, and natural marvels with comfort and convenience.

Amelia Island Travel Insurance

When planning a trip to Amelia Island, consider travel insurance as a crucial part of your travel preparations. While Amelia Island is recognized for its safety and friendliness, unforeseen occurrences may occur on every vacation.

Having comprehensive travel insurance not only protects you financially, but it also gives you peace of mind, enabling you to enjoy your holiday to the fullest.

Coverage for Trip Cancellation and Interruption:

Travel insurance covers trip cancellation or interruption caused by unanticipated events such as sickness, accident, or other crises. If you have to cancel or shorten your vacation due to a covered cause, travel insurance may compensate you for non-refundable charges such as airfare, lodging, and planned activities.

Medical Expenses and Evacuation in an Emergency:

Medical expenditures incurred during your vacation to Amelia Island are often covered by travel insurance. This coverage protects you financially in the event of sickness or accident while on the island. Furthermore, if a medical emergency necessitates evacuation to a higher level of care or back to your native country, travel insurance may cover the expenses of emergency medical evacuation.

Coverage for Baggage and Personal Effects:

Travel insurance may cover luggage and personal possessions that are lost, stolen, or destroyed. This includes payment for the expense of replacing necessary things such as clothes, toiletries, and gadgets that were stolen or damaged during your vacation.

Coverage for Travel Delays and Missed Connections:

If your journey to Amelia Island is delayed or you miss a connecting flight due to unforeseen circumstances, travel insurance may cover extra expenditures such as food, lodging, and transportation. This guarantees that unforeseen delays or missed connections do not cost you money.

Emergency Services:

Most travel insurance policies provide 24-hour emergency help. This means you may get expert help and support in the event of an emergency, a medical consultation, or a travel-related problem. Emergency assistance services are just a phone call away if you need aid locating medical facilities, scheduling transportation, or addressing travel-related concerns.

Coverage for Pre-Existing Medical Conditions:

If you have pre-existing medical illnesses, you must choose a travel insurance plan that covers these conditions. When getting travel insurance, be careful to mention any pre-existing ailments to ensure that you are sufficiently covered in the event of any relevant medical difficulties during your trip.

Optional Extra Coverage:

Travel insurance often includes extra coverage choices that may be customized to your unique requirements. These choices may include rental automobile coverage, adventure sports coverage, or personal liability coverage. Examine the insurance details carefully and pick any extra coverage choices that correspond to your planned activities on Amelia Island.

In conclusion, Purchasing Amelia Island travel insurance is a prudent option that will offer you with necessary safety and peace of mind during your vacation. Travel insurance protects you financially in the event of an unforeseen incident, from trip cancellation and interruption coverage to medical expenditures and emergency help.

Examine the policy terms, coverage limitations, and exclusions carefully before getting travel insurance to verify that it matches your personal requirements. You may experience the beauty of Amelia Island with confidence if you have travel insurance in place, knowing that you are prepared for any unexpected events that may happen.

Conclusion

As we near the conclusion of our tour of Amelia Island, it's evident that this enthralling place has a universe of treasures waiting to be explored.

Amelia Island, with its beautiful beaches and magnificent sunsets, as well as its rich history and dynamic culture, makes an unforgettable imprint on every tourist who is lucky enough to witness its beauty.

Amelia Island's attractiveness stems not only from its beautiful scenery, but also from the kindness and friendliness of its inhabitants. With their welcoming grins and genuine charm, the people make tourists feel like they are a part of the island's fabric. Their tales, handed down through generations, give a vivid picture of the island's history and the many forces that have influenced it.

Fernandina Beach, Amelia Island's historic center, is a treasure trove of architectural wonders and hidden beauties. The well-preserved Victorian-era buildings and vibrant stores entice tourists to discover their mysteries. Walking around the ancient streets transports you back in time, envisioning the stories that unfold behind the walls of these storied buildings.

Amelia Island is a haven of peace and spectacular beauty for nature enthusiasts. The lush vegetation, meandering pathways, and plentiful animals create an amazing setting for outdoor excursions.

Nature's embrace is ever-present, whether kayaking along the beautiful rivers, trekking through the island's parks, or just relaxing on its beaches.

But Amelia Island is more than simply a sensory experience; it is also a gastronomic heaven. The island's cuisine is a wonderful joy, from exquisite seafood fished fresh from the water to the tastes of the South that dazzle taste senses. Each taste reveals a mix of flavors that reflects the island's rich cultural background as well as its prominence as a culinary destination.

As my time visiting Amelia Island draws to an end, I've reflected on the memories I've made, the tales I've heard, and the beauty I've seen. It is a location that catches the mind and leaves a lasting memory that persists long after one has left.

Amelia Island has a particular place in the hearts of those who have experienced its beauty, whether it's the sound of breaking waves, the fragrance of salt in the air, or the feeling of history engraved into every cobblestone.

So, if you're looking for a location that combines natural beauty, historical history, and a warm welcome, go no further than Amelia Island. It is a location where dreams are realized, memories are formed, and the spirit of adventure can be found at every turn. Set foot on this enchanting island and let its beauty wash over you, for Amelia Island is more than simply a location on a map—it is an experience that will last a lifetime.

Printed in Great Britain
by Amazon

26281549R00089